ROY BENNETT
formerly Head of Music and Drama at
Buckler's Mead School, Yeovil

Enjoying music

BOOK 2

LONGMAN

How an orchestra is laid out.

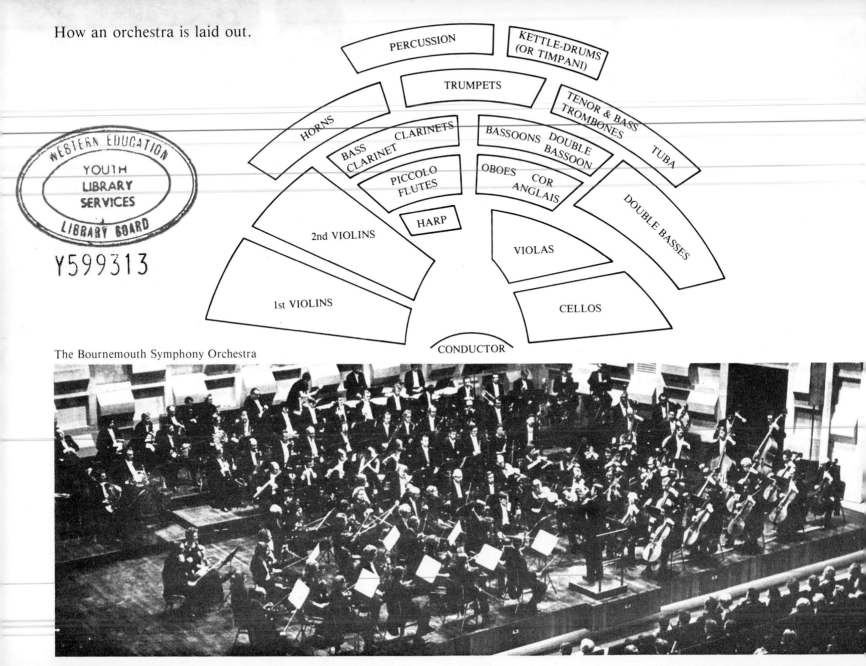

PERCUSSION

KETTLE-DRUMS (OR TIMPANI)

TRUMPETS

TENOR & BASS TROMBONES

HORNS

CLARINETS

BASSOONS DOUBLE BASSOON

TUBA

BASS CLARINET

PICCOLO FLUTES

OBOES COR ANGLAIS

DOUBLE BASSES

2nd VIOLINS

HARP

VIOLAS

1st VIOLINS

CELLOS

CONDUCTOR

The Bournemouth Symphony Orchestra

Gustav Holst ENGLAND 1874-1934

'Mars', 'Venus' and 'Jupiter'

from The Planets

Holst's great-grandfather came from Sweden to settle in England in the year 1807. Holst himself was born in 1874, two years later than another great English composer, Vaughan Williams. Both men were very interested in English folk music, and became close friends. Originally Holst had wanted to become a pianist, but neuritis in his hands forced him to give up the piano. Instead, he took up the trombone, and gained valuable musical experience by playing in an orchestra. Just after the turn of the century he gave up playing to take charge of music at St. Paul's Girls School in London, using all his spare time to write music. It was for the orchestra of this school that he composed the *St. Paul's Suite for Strings*.

Astrologers have always believed that the movements and relative positions of the planets have a direct influence on men's lives. The Romans named each known planet after one of their gods. For example, a planet glowing with an angry, reddish light was called Mars after the Roman god of war, and was thought to have a violent and war-like influence.

About the year 1913, Holst became very interested in astrology. He wrote in a letter:

'As a rule I only study things that suggest music to me . . . Then recently the character of each planet suggested lots to me, and I have been studying astrology fairly closely.'

He wrote a *suite* (or group) of seven pieces, each based on one of the planets, for a huge orchestra of over a hundred players. Each piece had the name of a planet, and a sub-title as well.

If any guide to the music is required the subtitle to each piece will be found sufficient especially if used in its broadest sense.

Mars, the Bringer of War

This first piece from *The Planets* was written early in the summer of 1914, a few weeks before the outbreak of the First World War. Although Holst can have had no idea of the horrors that were to follow, this music has been described as 'a prophecy of the mechanised warfare which was to come . . .'

Points to listen for

1. Kettle-drum, harps and strings (played *col legno* — 'with the wood' of the bow instead of the hair) beat out a relentless rhythm **(A)**. The unusual number of beats to each bar makes the rhythm all the more insistent. Against this, horns and bassoons play a menacing figure which rises five notes, then falls back a note **(B)**.
2. Brass fanfares and screams from the woodwind are heard — and

Gustav Holst

3

the rhythm is hammered out even more forcefully. A slithering theme, first introduced by trombones and tuba (**C**), gradually builds to a climax.

3. The rhythm changes to a steady, pounding beat on the strings. Then a fanfare-like theme is played by the tenor tuba, answered by a flourish of trumpets (**D**).

4. More and more instruments join in as the tension gradually builds up. Trumpets, snare-drum and a long roll on the cymbal are followed by a scurrying passage — first downwards, then up — then a crashing chord which gradually dies away.

5. Theme **C** slithers about desolately — less loud, but just as menacing. From the gloom and confusion, occasional muffled drum-beats and trumpet-calls emerge.

6. The music desperately tries to drag itself upwards, higher and higher. The 5-beat rhythm is hammered out by brass and snare-drum, and theme **B** returns with renewed strength.

7. The tension builds almost to breaking-point. Theme **C** is followed by savage discords marked *ffff* and reinforced by organ.

8. For one brief moment the tension is relaxed. Another scurrying passage — and the entire force of the huge orchestra is hurled into an irregular rhythmic pounding. Then — total collapse.

In this music there is to be found none of the pageantry or the 'glory' of war - only the desperation and empty futility.

Venus, the Bringer of Peace

This hushed, flowing music offers a complete contrast to the desperation and savage brutality of 'Mars'.

Points to listen for

1. Four smooth rising notes from a horn are answered by the cool, liquid tone of flutes and oboes. A gentle rocking rhythm begins.

2. From a long-sustained note on the violins emerges the sound of a single violin, serene and consoling (**E**), against soft, throbbing chords. Then the other violins take up the theme.

3. There are other solos, especially for the oboe.

4. Eventually, the rocking rhythm returns and the opening music is heard again.

5. Theme **E** on violins, high and silvery.

6. The last moments suggest the hushed darkness and the timeless quality of space. Listen for the sparkling sounds of the glockenspiel and celesta.

Examples of how seventeenth century men thought of the planets — Venus (left) and Jupiter (right)

4

French horn

violin

Jupiter, the Bringer of Jollity

Jupiter was the ruler of the gods. He was also known as Jove, from which we get the word 'jovial', meaning 'jolly'. That is why Holst gave the planet Jupiter the title 'the Bringer of Jollity'.

Holst's music with its sparkling melodies, explosive chords, and dancing rhythms, gives a vivid impression of good humour and high spirits. The first time that 'Jupiter' was tried over by an orchestra, the cleaning women threw down their scrubbing-brushes in the corridors outside the concert hall and danced to its rhythms! These rhythms rely a great deal on *syncopation* - an exciting rhythmic effect in which emphasis is placed on weak beats rather than strong.

Points to listen for

1. Violins play a dancing, background accompaniment woven from the opening notes of theme **H** marked '*x*'. (This scrap of tune is important, and will be heard again and again in the music.) Against this: a syncopated theme (**F**) — first on horns, violas and cellos; then, more loudly, on brass, low woodwind and double basses.

2. Horns announce the second theme (**G**). The first bar — rising four notes, then four notes again — is also important, and will be heard frequently later on.

3. Theme **H**, a vigorous dance, is given to strings and horns. It is immediately repeated by the woodwind with sparkling touches from the glockenspiel.

4. So far, every theme has had two beats to each bar. The next though is in three-time (**I**). It is heard six times, each time with different, colourful orchestration.

5. A blazing fanfare from the heavy brass, and fragments of tune **H** on woodwind instruments prepare the way for a broad string melody (**J**) which seems to remind us that, besides bringing jollity, Jupiter was also the dignified ruler of the gods. (This melody is sometimes sung to the words 'I vow to thee, my country'.) Notice that this melody, like theme **H**, also begins with the important little figure marked '*x*'.

6. The jovial mood returns and all the previous themes reappear in new orchestral colours. Listen, towards the end, for a reminder of the dignified broad melody (**J**).

The remaining movements in *The Planets* are: Mercury, the Winged Messenger; Saturn, the Bringer of Old Age; Uranus, the Magician; and Neptune, the Mystic. The orchestra for *The Planets* needs: 4 flutes, 2 piccolos, bass flute, 3 oboes, cor anglais, 3 clarinets, bass clarinet, 3 bassoons, double bassoon, 6 horns, 4 trumpets, 3 trombones, 2 tubas, 2 harps, percussion, organ and strings, with a female choir in the last piece.

Pomp and Circumstance Marches 1 and 4

Many musicians spend years learning about their craft from a teacher — either privately, or in a college or university. Elgar taught himself. His father was an organist and kept a music shop in Worcester (not far from the Malvern Hills), so the boy had plenty of encouragement.

He would try out the instruments his father sold, and in this way eventually taught himself to play the piano, violin, viola, bassoon, and organ. Soon he was deputising for his father at the church organ, playing the bassoon in a local wind group, and the violin in an amateur orchestra. Later on he became the conductor of the orchestra of a nearby lunatic asylum.

Elgar's ambition was to become a composer. Unfortunately, there was no money to pay for expensive lessons — so once again he became his own teacher. He married, and went to live in London. But he found it very difficult to make a reputation — there had been no truly great English composer for more than 200 years.

Elgar left London and settled in Malvern, in the countryside he knew from his boyhood. Here he wrote several short, tuneful pieces, including *Chanson de Matin* (Morning Song), and *Chanson de Nuit* (Night Song), and the beautiful *Serenade for Strings*. But it was not until his *Enigma Variations* were performed in London in 1899 that Elgar really achieved success. In this music, each variation is a musical picture of one of Elgar's friends - including someone who was keen on amateur dramatics, a peppery country squire, an organist with a particularly boisterous bulldog, and the final variation is a musical portrait of the composer himself.

In 1901, Elgar wrote the first of the five marches which he called *Pomp and Circumstance,* inspired by the coronation of King Edward VII. The orchestration was brilliantly colourful, and this time the melodies went straight to the heart of the listener. By now he had won recognition as a composer of world fame and it was suggested that it was 'undignified for a composer of Elgar's stature to write marches'. Elgar firmly replied:

'I know that there are a lot of people who like to celebrate events with music. To these people I have given tunes. Is that wrong? Why should I write a fugue *or something that won't appeal to anyone, when people yearn for things which can stir them?'*

The coronation procession of King Edward VII

No.1 in D Major

1. A short, blazing introduction.
2. The rhythmic theme of the *March* (**A**) is given mainly to the strings, with colourful sounds from the percussion section — especially snare-drum, cymbals, triangle and kettle-drums. Later, there is exciting work for trumpets and trombones.
3. Soft-treading chords introduce the *Trio,* or contrasting section. This melody (**B**) was also used by Elgar in his *Coronation Ode* written the same year, 1901. A verse, beginning 'Land of Hope and Glory', was set to the tune, and is now always associated with this march (although Elgar himself did not like the association). The melody is first played *piano* (softly) by violins; then repeated *forte* (loudly) an octave higher and strengthened by brass with snare-drum and cymbals. (Notice that the main notes of both themes, **A** and **B**, descend one step at a time.)
4. The *March* returns.
5. Then the *Trio* follows as a climax to the whole piece, now played very stirringly with percussive clashes on each beat.
6. A reminder of the *March* theme brings the music to an exciting finish, with glittering sounds from the glockenspiel.

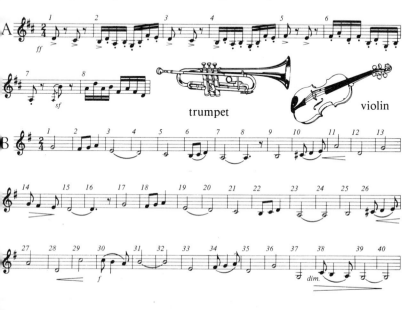

trumpet

violin

No. 4 in G Major

Apart from having no introduction, the fourth march is very similar to the first in design and orchestration.

1. The *March* section has a confident, rhythmic theme (**C**).
2. Elgar hits on a theme for the *Trio* section (**D**) which is almost as broad and lyrical as the famous melody from *March No. 1*. He deals with it in exactly the same way: softly first, on violins; then loudly, an octave higher, with brass and snare-drum.
3. The rhythmic *March* tune returns.
4. The flowing melody of the *Trio* is heard again, as climax to the piece, with forceful chords on every beat.
5. A *coda,* or ending, reminds us of the *March* theme.

'Land of Hope and Glory,
Mother of the free,
How shall we extol thee
Who are born of thee?
Wider still and wider
Shall thy bounds be set.
God who made thee mighty,
Make thee mightier yet!'

Pomp and Circumstance March No. 1 is played at the last night of the Promenade Concerts in London each summer. The entire audience joins in by singing the words. When he wrote this piece, Elgar said:

I've a tune that will knock 'em flat … a tune like that comes once in a lifetime.

Franz Liszt HUNGARY 1811-1886

Hungarian Rhapsody No. 2

Hungarian folk dancing

Hungary lies in the very heart of Europe — a vast plain surrounded by hills and mountains and crossed by the river Danube.

Hungary has two kinds of 'folk' music — the music of the peasants and gypsy music. The true peasant songs and dances have only become known to the rest of the world in this century. Before that, the music thought of as Hungarian folk music was the kind played by gypsy musicians — music alternately slow and mournful, and quick and fiery, with a great many runs, trills, flourishes and other decorations. It was these tunes which were used by Liszt in his *Hungarian Rhapsodies*. (A *rhapsody* is a piece in which there is no very firm structure, with exciting contrasts, and very colourful orchestration.)

Liszt's *Hungarian Rhapsodies* were first written for piano. Later, he scored six of them for orchestra. Liszt went to stay with the Hungarian gypsies in order to study their music:

'We were living with them — right among them. We slept with them under the open starry sky, played with their children, chatted with the old folk. We listened to their music in the glow of the gypsy camp-fire . . .'

Liszt was possibly the most brilliant pianist the world has ever known — some people even suggested he had made a pact with the devil in return for such amazing technique! He quickly became a public idol. Women especially admired him for both his striking looks and his incredible piano-playing. He was treated in very much the same way as a 'pop' singer might be nowadays. One lady, usually very particular about personal cleanliness, was noticed by her friends to smell rather offensively. Eventually, when she died, it was discovered that she had acquired one of Liszt's cigar stumps as a souvenir 25 years earlier, and placed it lovingly in her corsage where it had remained ever since! Sometimes his relationships with women made life difficult. In 1834 he eloped with the Countess Marie d'Agoult, a woman who was to live with him for the next ten years and bear him three children. This event caused such public scandal in Paris, where Liszt was living at the time, that all the time the relationship lasted he was forced to roam Europe in exile, as polite society in France would not accept him.

Very often Liszt played his own music at concerts, or his arrangements of pieces by other composers — orchestral works, songs and operatic fantasias. He was often in the company of men who were in the public eye: other composers such as Berlioz and Chopin, and leaders of the Romantic Movement in literature such as the French poets Lamartine and Victor Hugo. It may have been these associations which led him to write orchestral *tone poems* — music which tells a story or paints a picture in sound, such as Saint-Saëns's *Danse Macabre* or Smetana's *Vltava*. Liszt was always willing to help other composers to make their reputation. In particular, he helped Grieg, Dvořák, Borodin, Tchaikovsky, and Wagner (who later became his son-in-law).

Points to listen for

The *Rhapsody No. 2* is in two sections, each based upon the rhythms of the Hungarian dance called the *Czardas* — the slow step, known as the *lassan* (or sometimes *lassu);* and the quick step, known as the *friska* (or *friss*).

1. First a slow, solemn introduction, eight bars long, richly scored for low-pitched violins, violas and clarinets (**A**) with weighty off-beat chords for lower strings and brass.

2. *Lassan:* this section makes much use of a mournful melody for strings and clarinets (**B**), with a heavy accompaniment.

3. In the middle of this section there is a hint of theme **C** (to be heard more brilliantly in the *friska* later) scored for piccolo, flute, harp and violas, with triangle and glockenspiel. The pace is slightly faster.

4. Listen for reappearances of the introductory theme (**A**) and especially for three passages for clarinet *solo* suggesting the very free, decorative flourishes of a gypsy musician.

5. *Friska*: really a string of colourful and exciting gypsy melodies. First, theme **C** on the oboe with violin accompaniment and 'chirps' from other woodwind instruments.

6. A passage marked *crescendo* (gradually louder) and *accelerando* (gradually faster) launches into the exciting main theme (**D**), played by the full orchestra.

7. Listen for a hint of theme **F** (to be heard more definitely later on) played by strings in *syncopation* (an exciting rhythmic effect with notes emphasised *off*-the-beat).

8. The pace is pulled back for a moment as violins play theme **E** — but this, too, gets gradually faster.

9. The brass blares out theme **F**, with *syncopated* accompaniment.

10. Cellos introduce theme **G**, and the dance gets wilder and even more exciting as the brass brings in theme **F** again.

11. Then a pause — as clarinet and bassoon remind us of the mournful mood of the *lassan*.

12. Finally, a very fast *coda* (or ending) on theme **G**, beginning *pianissimo,* but working up gradually to *fortissimo*.

I could not write about my own life. I was always too busy living it!

The clarinet

This woodwind instrument has a *single reed,* a flat piece of cane fixed to the mouthpiece by a metal band. The player's breath causes this reed to vibrate (rather like a piece of grass held between the thumbs).

The lower notes of the clarinet sound rather hollow, but rich and velvety. In the middle register the notes are smooth, while in the higher register the notes are more piercing. The instrument has a very wide range of expression.

Although the clarinet was invented early in the 18th century, it didn't really find a place in the orchestra until Mozart began to write music for it.

The *bass clarinet* is shaped very like a saxophone. It can play lower notes than the ordinary clarinet, and the tone is richer and darker.

9

Manuel de Falla SPAIN 1876-1946
Two Dances from
The Three-Cornered Hat

Andalusian landscape

The music which people think of as typically Spanish comes from one particular region of Spain called Andalusia. In the eighth century, Moors (or Arabs) came from North Africa to conquer Southern Spain, remaining there for several centuries. Gypsies came from Central Europe and settled there as well — so besides having a typically Spanish flavour, the folk music of Andalusia also has Arab and gypsy ingredients.

During the last hundred years, Spain has produced three great composers: Isaac Albéniz, Enrique Granados, and Manuel de Falla (pronounced *'Fal-*ya'). All three took lessons with the same teacher, Felipe Pedrell. At that time, most Spanish music was written in the form of light entertainments called *zarzuelas* — comic plays with music. Pedrell wanted composers to write music of a more serious nature — but music which still reflected the character of Spain. Manuel de Falla made up his mind to do just that.

He went to Paris, intending to stay for only one week — but he remained there for seven years! He became friendly with two great French composers, Debussy and Ravel. At the outbreak of the First World War, in 1914, he returned to Spain. The years in France had taught him a great deal about composing music, and orchestration. Now, having soaked himself in the folk music of his native country, Falla wrote a work for piano and orchestra, full of mystery and atmosphere, which he called *Nights in the Gardens of Spain*. Two ballets followed: *Love the Magician* (from which comes the exciting 'Ritual Fire Dance'), and *The Three-Cornered Hat*. All this music was thoroughly Spanish in flavour, yet, apart from two brief tunes in *The Three-Cornered Hat,* all the melodies were Falla's own. As he pointed out: 'My aim was to write genuine Spanish music without using actual folk-songs.'

The 'three-cornered hat' is worn by the magistrate of a small town as his symbol of office. This foolish old man tries, unsuccessfully, to flirt with the miller's wife while the miller is away. For the first production the great Spanish artist, Pablo Picasso, designed the scenery and costumes. The part of the miller was danced by the famous dancer, Massine, who was also the choreographer. (A choreographer works out the dances and tells the dancers which steps to use.) In this ballet, Massine used only the authentic steps of Spanish dances.

Neighbours' Dance

It is night — warm, starlit and mysterious. The miller, his wife and their neighbours perform a rhythmic, flowing dance. The music makes great use of a melody which gently surges from *pianissimo* to *forte* (**A**). There are two other tunes: a rhythmic theme for strings (**B**); and a melody for flute and bassoon (**C**) which is a kind of Spanish dance known as a *seguidilla*.

The Miller's Dance

The miller dances a *farruca* to entertain his neighbours. A *farruca* is an Andalusian gypsy dance which calls for both skill and stamina. There is a great deal of leaping, twisting and slick heel-tapping. The scene is set by solos for horn (**D**) and cor anglais (**E**). The dance proper begins 'at a very moderate pace, rhythmically and heavily' (**F**). Here, the entire string section imitates the crashing chords of a gigantic guitar, while the following oboe melody suggests the nasal voice of a Spanish singer (**G**). A stealthy passage for lower strings and woodwind (**H**) leads back to the crashing chords (**I**). We hear theme **G** played by the horn, then the dance concludes with an exciting *coda* — stamping chords which grow gradually faster and louder to the end. (Picture on the left.)

When you listen to these dances, notice how Falla cleverly combines and contrasts groups of instruments, and uses exciting rhythms to make his music sound truly Spanish.

French horn   oboe
                     cor anglais

11

Joaquin Rodrigo SPAIN born 1902

Concierto de Aranjuez

for guitar and orchestra

Joaquin Rodrigo was born in Valencia, a town in the East of Spain on the Mediterranean Coast. Valencia was once the capital of the Moorish part of Spain.

At the age of three, Rodrigo went blind. But this did not prevent him from studying music — first in Valencia, later in Paris. When he returned to Spain, he settled in Madrid. It was there that he wrote the *concerto* for guitar and orchestra which he called *Concierto de Aranjuez*. In a *concerto*, the sound of a single instrument, or small group of instruments, is contrasted against the more powerful sound of an orchestra.

At first, people were afraid the solo guitar would be overpowered by the orchestra. But when they heard the music, they discovered that the composer had used great skill and imagination in balancing his unequal forces. Sometimes the guitar is accompanied by the orchestra, and sometimes there is a kind of 'dialogue' between the two. There are even occasions when the guitar plays an accompaniment to the orchestra, or a group of instruments drawn from it.

Concierto de Aranjuez quickly became very popular because of its catchy melodies and spontaneous rhythms. Though these are of Rodrigo's own invention, they have all the exciting flavour of Spanish folk melodies and dance rhythms.

Aranjuez is the ancient palace of the kings of Spain, set among beautiful parks and gardens in the valley of the River Tagus between Madrid and Toledo.

My concerto is meant to sound like the hidden breeze which stirs the tree-tops in the parks. It should be as strong as a butterfly...

The guitar
Besides the castanets, the instrument which we associate most with Spain is the guitar. It is a very old instrument, dating back at least to the 14th century. Then, it had only four strings; now there are usually six. The fingerboard has metal *frets,* telling the player where to place his fingers on the strings to obtain the notes.

The guitar is capable of producing extremely varied sounds, ranging from a soft plaintive tone to exciting, crashing chords. Rodrigo describes his ideal guitar as 'a strange, fantastic instrument with the wings of a harp, the tail of a piano, and a soul of its own'.

1. Allegro con spirito (lively and with spirit)
1.   Above a soft low D, sustained by double basses, the guitar strums a rhythm **(A)** — gradually growing louder, then softer again. Notice how the accents of the rhythm change from $\frac{6}{8}$ (six quavers to each bar with *two* strong beats) to $\frac{3}{4}$ (three crotchets to each bar, with *three* strong beats). The mixing of these rhythms (known as *cross-rhythms*) is typical of Spanish music.
2.   The guitar plays a clear, straight-forward tune **(B)**.
3.   Strings take over the opening rhythm **(A)** which now becomes an

Spot the guitar in Picasso's *Three Musicians* (left)!

accompaniment to a melody danced by the violins (**C**).

4. Tune **B**, played by the orchestra, leads into a theme for the guitar (**D**). There are fresh, clear sounds from the woodwind instruments (rather like bird-songs), and *pizzicato* (plucked) notes from the violins.

5. Four bars of stamping, rhythmic chords (which become important later) introducing another melody for the guitar (**E**).

6. The *development section* (where some of these ideas are 'developed' or worked out) begins with a solo cello playing theme **C** in the key of A minor. When the violins played this dance-like theme earlier, the key was D *major;* by putting it into the *minor* key, and giving it to the cello, Rodrigo makes it sound darker and rather plaintive. The theme is passed to other instruments alternating with a fragment of theme **D** (marked '*x*'). There are loudly strummed chords and brilliant running passages for the guitar, and much is made of the stamping chords with their exciting 'cross-rhythms'. The development section ends with the flickering scale which ends theme **B**.

7. The opening rhythm comes again (**A**) while violins play theme **C**, in the major key. To this, the guitar immediately adds the second half of theme **D** (bar 7 onwards).

8. The stamping 'cross-rhythms' again introduce theme **E**: played first by the clarinet, while the guitar accompanies; then by the guitar.

9. While the strings play tune **B**, the woodwind remind us of tune **C**.

10. Exciting sounds from the full orchestra and rhythmic strummings on the guitar. Then the movement fades to a quiet close — tune **B**, followed by the 'cross-rhythms' with which the music first began (**A**).

2. Adagio (slowly)

1. The guitar accompanies a melody on the cor anglais (**F**). There are two long phrases, each repeated by the guitar with a great deal of decoration. There is a tender sadness in this music, and also some of the mystery of music of the night.

2. Phrases from the orchestra are interrupted by free, almost improvisatory, patterns from the guitar.

3. First *cadenza*. (In a *cadenza,* the orchestra remains silent while the soloist shows off his technique with some dazzling playing.) The guitar laments upon the theme, providing its own accompaniment.

4. The oboe is answered by more intricate patterns on the guitar. A brief orchestral outburst.

5. Second *cadenza*. Fragments of the theme above repeated notes,

becoming more excited and leading to:

6. A passionate version of the theme by the full orchestra. Then the music ends quietly.

3. Allegro gentile

The last movement of the concerto is based on a single theme (**G**) which alternates between 2 and 3 beats to a bar. It comes round over and over, and each time it seems to be played by a different combination of instruments. As in the first movement, the rhythms are gay and lively, but Rodrigo also marks this music *gentile* (gentle, or delicately) as if remembering the old stately Spanish court dances as they would have been performed in the palace of Aranjuez.

13

Georges Bizet FRANCE 1838-1875

Music from **Carmen**

In the 19th century, several composers outside Spain — especially in France and Russia — became very interested in the folk music of Spain. They composed a great deal of 'Spanish' music, using the rhythms of Spanish dances and typical Spanish instruments such as the castanets and tambourine. The French composer, Chabrier, wrote a vivid piece for orchestra which he called *España* (Spain); Ravel composed a *Bolero;* and the Russian, Rimsky-Korsakov, wrote *Capriccio Espagnol.* But the best-known music in this style is Bizet's colourful opera, *Carmen.*

At first *Carmen* was not a success with the Paris audiences. Perhaps they wanted a happy ending. Certainly they must have been taken aback by the fiery, flashing-eyed gypsy girl who is the main character, for before the creation of Carmen, operatic heroines had usually been rather pale, well-bred ladies.

The story
Brightly uniformed soldiers mingle with the bustling townsfolk in the crowded public square of Seville, in the South of Spain. Carmen, a wild and beautiful gypsy-girl who works in the nearby cigarette factory, picks a quarrel with another girl and wounds her with a knife. She is arrested by a young corporal of the Dragoons named Don José, but he is so fascinated by her charm that he allows her to escape. For this 'carelessness' he is imprisoned.

When Don José is released, he meets Carmen at a tavern near the border. There, she and her gypsy friends persuade him to desert from the army and join their smuggling activities in the mountains. Carmen quickly tires of her new lover, however, and falls in love with a handsome toreador called Escamillo. Don José is overcome with jealousy. He receives a message that his mother is dying and reluctantly leaves for his native village.

While he is gone, Carmen returns to Seville, where Escamillo is to fight in the bull-ring. As she is about to enter the stadium, Don José appears and protests his love for her. But she merely laughs at his jealousy. Driven to desperation, he draws a dagger and stabs her. As Carmen sinks, dying, to the ground the victorious Escamillo returns from the arena, to the wild cheering of the excited crowd.

1. **Prelude to Act 1**

It is thought that Bizet composed the Prelude to *Carmen* after the opera was completed. He uses music which will be heard later in the opera, setting the mood and atmosphere for what is to follow.
1. First, the music of the Toreadors as they enter the arena for the bull-fight **(A)**. Kettle-drums, cymbals and triangle provide some exciting sounds.

Carmen and Don José, the corporal of the Dragoons (Act I)

I have written a work that is all clarity and vivacity, full of colour and melody. Come along — I think you will like it!

Bizet said
to a friend

14

A

2. There is a short contrasting theme for violins **(B)**, then we hear the first tune again.

3. Trumpets and trombones mark the beat of the 'Toreador's Song' — sung in the opera by Escamillo, but played here by strings **(C)**. The melody is repeated more loudly and with the beat punched out more strongly; then the opening music is heard once more.

4. After a pause, a shuddering chord is heard on the strings and we hear the theme associated with Carmen herself **(D)**. Here, with muffled thumps on kettle-drums and *pizzicato* basses, it sounds foreboding — as if hinting at future tragedy.

2. Habañera (Act I)

This dance takes its name from Havana in Cuba, but probably came originally from Spain itself. Carmen sings the Habañera, then flings a rose to Don José to attract his attention. He pretends to ignore her.

1. Cellos set the *habañera* rhythm, which is very similar to the *tango*. The melody **(E)** is heard three times: first by violins, then by flute, and thirdly by oboe with tambourine, triangle and *pizzicato* (plucked) strings.

2. In the refrain, the violins again take the tune with loud, brilliant chords for full orchestra. This, too, is repeated, the melody played by the woodwind, with tambourine and *pizzicato* strings accompanying.

3. Entr'acte: Les Dragons d'Alcala

An entr'acte is music played between acts when the curtain is down. This one, called 'The Dragoons of Alcala' also serves as a *prelude* (or 'opening-piece') to Act II of the opera. (Alcala is a district of the town of Seville.) The music is in *ternary* (three-part) design — that is, the same music at the beginning and end, but with a contrasting section in the middle.

1. Two bassoons play the march-tune **(F)**, accompanied by a crisp rhythm on snare-drum and *pizzicato* strings.

2. In the middle section, strings and woodwind share the tune **(G)**.

3. When the first music returns, a clarinet plays the march-tune against a running bassoon accompaniment. Then violins and violas hold a soft chord as woodwind instruments play a phrase in turn — flute, oboe, clarinet and bassoon.

15

4. Danse Bohème (Act II)

Carmen and her gypsy friends perform a breathless whirling dance for a group of rough soldiers in a tavern.

1. The first theme (**H**) is given to two flutes with *pizzicato* strings suggesting the plucked accompaniment of a guitar.

2. A song-like melody (**I**) is played by oboes and clarinets, soon joined by a tambourine.

The gypsy dance in the tavern (above) Carmen with the toreador, Escamillo (left)

3. Tune **J** provides a refrain to the song.

4. As these themes are heard alternately, the pace increases and the orchestration becomes more and more colourful. Listen for tune **I** played by a trumpet with brilliant explosive sounds from the percussion.

There is a great deal of work for the instrument much associated with gypsies — the tambourine. Sometimes it is tapped gently, or shaken so that we hear the vibration of the jingles; sometimes it is hit vigorously or smacked with the flat of the hand.

16

5. Entr'acte

A gentle *prelude* before the exciting music of the smugglers (Act III).
1. A flute plays a haunting melody above harp accompaniment **(K)**.
2. The melody is repeated by a clarinet, and the flute adds a descant above a softly held chord on two violins, viola and two cellos. Two basses, *pizzicato,* mark the first beat of each bar.
3. Cor anglais and bassoon add their darker tone-colours, then give way to the strings.
4. The instruments of the woodwind, one by one, remind us of the first bar of the theme.

6. Aragonaise (a dance from the Province of Aragon)

This wild, exciting music introduces the fourth and final act of the opera, which take place outside the bull-ring in Seville.
1. A fiery introduction for full orchestra including the tambourine — which once again has much to do.
2. *Pizzicato* strings provide an accompaniment for a rather mournful oboe melody **(L)**.
3. The second theme is shared between woodwind and strings **(M)**.
4. Then violins play a sweeping melody with an arrogant rhythmic snap **(N)**.
5. The oboe melody returns, and the music grows gradually quieter till the end.

The death scene — Don José has just stabbed Carmen

> '*To me, this is in every sense a masterpiece . . . From beginning to end, it is charming and delightful. In it, one finds a number of striking harmonies and entirely new combinations of sounds . . . And what a wonderful subject for an opera! I am convinced that in about ten years, Carmen will have become the most popular opera in the world . . .*'
>
> (Tchaikovsky)

But Bizet never lived to see Tchaikovsky's prediction — that *Carmen* would become the most popular opera in the world — come true. *Carmen* was the last music he wrote. He died a few months after the first performance at the age of 37.

17

Nicholas Rimsky-Korsakov RUSSIA 1844-1908

Music from **Capriccio Espagnol**

(Spanish Caprice)

Some composers write down their music, then decide later on which instruments are to play it. Other composers think up their music, and the characteristic sounds of the instruments which are to play it come to mind at the same time. Whichever way it is, writing for full orchestra (or *orchestration,* as it is called) is an art which demands a thorough knowledge of every instrument and its capabilities.

An expert orchestrator will contrast and blend his instruments in various ways to achieve an interesting and well-balanced sound.

In the late 18th century, the orchestra contained relatively few instruments: two each of flutes, oboes, clarinets, bassoons, horns, and trumpets, with kettle-drums and strings (see page 53). But by the end of the 19th century many more instruments had crept in, and composers became even more interested in *orchestration* and the extremely varied tone-colours in which they could clothe their musical ideas.

One of the most brilliant and imaginative orchestrators at the time was a Russian composer called Rimsky-Korsakov. Rimsky-Korsakov was born in St. Petersburg, the city now known as Leningrad. He became a naval cadet at the age of twelve, and after his commission was stationed in St. Petersburg, where he shared rooms with another Russian composer, Mussorgsky. Both became members of a group of composers known as 'The Mighty Handful' — or simply 'The Russian Five'. None of these composers had received special musical training. In fact, one of their aims was to write music which was not restricted by musical rules. However, Rimsky-Korsakov soon disagreed about this, and began to study books about musical theory. At the age of 27, he became a professor at the Conservatory, or music college, in St. Petersburg. In 1887 Rimsky-Korsakov began to write a piece of music based on themes from a collection of Spanish folk music which he found. At first he intended it to be for violin and orchestra, but he soon decided to include solos — or *cadenzas,* as he called them — for other instruments as well. Sometimes these solos are for a single instrument; sometimes the instruments play in pairs, or in small groups.

Because of these solos — and the fact that every player in the orchestra often has difficult music to play — *Capriccio Espagnol* is rather like a *concerto* for full orchestra. The piece is written for: 2 flutes, piccolo, 2 oboes, cor anglais, 2 clarinets, bass clarinet, 2 bassoons, double bassoon; 4 horns, 2 trumpets, 3 trombones and tuba; kettle-drums, snare-drum, bass-drum, triangle, tambourine, cymbals and castanets; harp and strings.

The St. Petersburg estate where Rimsky-Korsakov d

Scena e Canto Gitano (Scene and Gypsy Song)

Here, Rimsky-Korsakov uses a folk tune from the province of Andalusia. The *Scene* consists of a series of *cadenzas* for a variety of instruments. The tone-colours are constantly changing so that we hear a rich and varied tapestry of instrumental sounds. It is as if the scene which Rimsky-Korsakov imagined was of a group of gypsies trying out snatches of the *Song (Canto)* on various instruments.

Points to listen for

1. *Cadenza I:* a crisp roll on the snare-drum introduces a *cadenza* for two trumpets and four horns (**A**), based on the Gypsy Song to be heard later. The cadenza ends with a brilliant fanfare.

2. *Cadenza II:* the roll on the snare-drum becomes quieter, then continues to accompany a cadenza for solo violin (**B**).

3. Kettle-drum, snare-drum and cymbals set up a rhythm (**C**). They are soon joined by violins, alternately played *arco* (with the bow) and *pizzicato*. Above this rhythm rides the theme of the *Song,* played by solo flute and solo clarinet (**D**).

4. *Cadenza III:* the rhythm dissolves into a roll on a kettle-drum to accompany a cadenza for solo flute (**E**).

5. *Cadenza IV:* now a roll on a suspended cymbal with sponge-headed sticks, and we hear a cadenza for clarinet (**F**).

6. As the clarinet holds its final note, triangle and bassoons accompany a solo oboe playing the second phrase of the *Song* (**G**).

7. *Cadenza V:* the final, glittering cadenza is for harp and triangle, ending with sweeping harp *glissandos* in which the player brushes his hands in circular movements across the strings (**H**).

8. Fiercely-bowed violins introduce a new idea, excitingly punctuated by trombones, tuba and cymbals (**I**). Then the rhythm is really set going as violins play the *Gypsy Song.* The music of this section is repeated at a higher pitch.

9. A solo cello weeps over a melancholy theme (**J**) while an oboe plays the second phrase of the *Song.*

10. Theme **I** is heard on flute and oboe while the violins pluck their strings *quasi guitarra* — 'like a guitar'. The music becomes even more colourful and exciting, with snare-drum rolls, cymbal clashes and rippling sounds from the harp.

11. The *Song* is heard on the woodwind against sweeping violins.

12. We hear the *Song* once more on the violins, then theme **I**, with brilliant harp *glissandos,* leads straight into the *Fandango Asturiano.*

Fandango Asturiano

The gypsies dance a lively *fandango.* Here, Rimsky-Korsakov gives his music a truly Spanish flavour by including castanets. There are two themes: the first is given to trombones and tuba, then taken over by woodwind and castanets (**K**); the second is played by cellos and bassoons (**L**). But the second part of theme **K** is heard most often. Towards the end of this short piece the excitement increases as we hear the main themes of the Caprice one after the other. First the *Gypsy Song* (trumpet); then the *Fandango* (trombones and tuba); and finally the colourful *Alborada* with which the whole work begins.

castanets
cymbals
snare-drum
triangle
trumpet

Quiz 1

1. Fill in the dashes

Fill in the dashes to discover six composers. Then give the nationality of each one.

a) B-Z-T d) -L-A-
b) H-L-T e) -A-L-
c) L-S-T f) R-D-I-O

Fill in the dashes here to discover six instruments. Then give the section of the orchestra to which each one belongs.

g) P-C-O-O j) -L-R-N-T
h) C-L-O k) -R-A-G-E
i) T-U-P-T l) M-R-C-S

2. Any other name . . .

Can you match each composer's christian name to the correct surname? Then give a piece of music written by each one.

Gustav   Bizet
Nicholas   Elgar
Georges   Liszt
Edward   Holst
Franz   Rimsky-Korsakov

3. In plain English . . .

Can you give the English meaning for each of these Italian words?

a) Forte   d) Cadenza   g) Arco
b) Piano   e) Crescendo h) Col legno
c) Coda   f) Pizzicato i) Tremolo

4. Which instrument

Here are some anagrams — or jumbled words. Each one is an instrument.

a) Cop coil   e) Cast eel

20

b) On a boss   f) Let trek mud
c) Holy ox pen   g) Rain celt
d) A tub   h) Be bad souls

5. More anagrams

These are jumbled countries. Can you name composers from each one?

a) Pains   c) Graynuh
b) Atairus   d) Valsekochzoica

6. Which section?

To which sections of the orchestra do these instruments belong?

a) Viola   d) Clarinet   g) Tambourine
b) Cello   e) Bassoon   h) Cor anglais
c) Harp   f) Snare-drum i) Glockenspiel

7. Composer and country

Decode the following to discover 5 composers and 5 countries. Then arrange them in matching pairs, each composer next to his country. Can you name a piece of music by each composer? (The code is A=1, B=2, C=3)

a) 8-21-14-7-1-18-25   f) 12-9-19-26-20
b) 8-15-12-19-20   g) 5-14-7-12-1-14-4
c) 19-16-1-9-14   h) 6-1-12-12-1
d) 2-9-26-5-20   i) 6-18-1-14-3-5
e) 18-21-19-19-9-1   j) 18-9-13-19-11-25-
                          11-15-18-19-1-11-
                          15-22

8. Who wrote . . . ?

Give the name and nationality of:

a) A composer who wrote a 'Spanish' opera.
b) A composer who wrote a Spanish Caprice.
c) A composer who wrote a Spanish ballet.
d) A composer who wrote Hungarian Rhapsodies.
e) A composer who wrote Hungarian Dances.

9. What am I?

a) I am a string instrument.
   I am one of the tallest instruments in the orchestra.
   I am never played with a bow.
b) I am from the brass section.
   I have no valves.
c) I am a wind instrument.
   I have a single reed.
   I am made of brass, not wood.
d) I am made of wood or metal.
   I am held sideways, and blown.
   I am the smallest instrument in my section.

10. Musical words

When you have answered these questions, take the first letter of each answer. The letters will spell another musical word.

A. a) Bowed string instrument.
   b) Italian for 'slowly'.
   c) Blind Spanish composer.
   d) Holst's 'Bringer of War'.
   e) English composer.
   f) Exciting dance from the ballet, 'The Three-Cornered Hat'.

B. a) Holst's nationality.
   b) Hungarian composer.
   c) Spanish stringed instrument.
   d) Operas are usually divided into these
   e) Russian composer known for his brilliant orchestration.

C. a) Liszt's nationality.
   b) Usually begins an opera.
   c) Elizabethan plucked instrument.
   d) Nationality of the composer of 'The Three-Cornered Hat'.
   e) Three-part design: A B A.

Medieval music-making

The word *medieval* means 'of the Middle Ages', or the period from the 12th century to around the middle of the 15th century.

It was a time when few people could afford to travel, to buy rich clothes or fine houses. So any opportunity was seized to enjoy the simple pleasures of singing, dancing, and making music.

Until recently, little was known about medieval music. Much of it has been lost — and, of course, the instruments which played it. But we are all the time discovering new pieces of information. As far as the instruments are concerned, we rely on pictures in old manuscripts, paintings and sculptures, wood-carvings, tapestries and stained-glass windows. And we find descriptions of many of the instruments in poems and chronicles written at the time.

Many musicians are now becoming very interested in the reconstruction of medieval instruments, so that the music which has survived is being played once more. People today are still enjoying the fresh melodies and lively rhythms of this 'old' music.

Medieval instruments — "loud" and "soft"

Medieval instruments were divided into two groups: 'loud' instruments for outdoor music, such as dancing, processions and public occasions; and 'soft' instruments for music indoors — dancing, song accompaniments, and 'background' music. Some instruments, by the kind of sound they made, could belong to both groups.

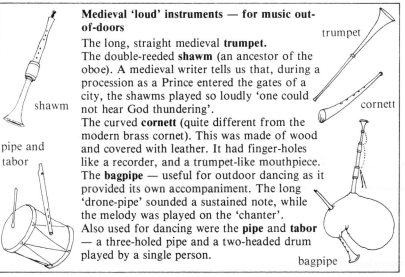

Medieval 'loud' instruments — for music out-of-doors

The long, straight medieval **trumpet**.

The double-reeded **shawm** (an ancestor of the oboe). A medieval writer tells us that, during a procession as a Prince entered the gates of a city, the shawms played so loudly 'one could not hear God thundering'.

The curved **cornett** (quite different from the modern brass cornet). This was made of wood and covered with leather. It had finger-holes like a recorder, and a trumpet-like mouthpiece.

The **bagpipe** — useful for outdoor dancing as it provided its own accompaniment. The long 'drone-pipe' sounded a sustained note, while the melody was played on the 'chanter'.

Also used for dancing were the **pipe** and **tabor** — a three-holed pipe and a two-headed drum played by a single person.

shawm

pipe and tabor

trumpet

cornett

bagpipe

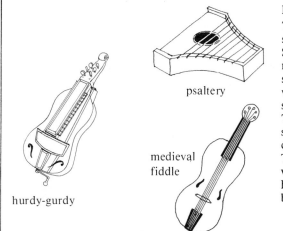

psaltery

medieval fiddle

hurdy-gurdy

Medieval 'soft' instruments — for music indoors

These included the long-necked **lute, recorders** of various sizes, and the soft-toned medieval **flute**.

Songs were often accompanied by the **minstrel's harp** (smaller than the modern harp, and with far fewer strings), or by the **psaltery**, whose strings were plucked with goose quills, one in each hand. The **dulcimer** was a very similar instrument, except the strings were beaten with sticks.

The **medieval fiddle** was slightly larger than the modern viola, and slightly lower in pitch. The bridge was fairly flat, so that two strings could easily be bowed at once.

The **hurdy-gurdy** was also a stringed instrument, but was not played with a bow. Instead, there was a rotating wooden wheel turned by a handle. The melody strings were 'stopped' by wooden sliders, pressed by the fingers, while the other strings sounded a drone.

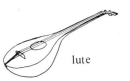

lute

minstrel's harp

1. Kalenda Maya: a troubadour song, by Raimbault de Vacqueiras

At the beginning of the 12th century, many songs were written by the *troubadours* — the poet-musicians of Southern France — and by the *trouvères*, their counterparts in the North. These songs would have been accompanied by instruments, but they are not mentioned in the manuscripts. Only the words and melodies are written down. The poems are often about nature, or the charms of fair ladies. 'Kalenda Maya' is a lively song about both. There are three phrases, each one repeated.

2. Ja Nun Hons Pris: a trouvère song, by Richard I, King of England

Richard I, nicknamed 'the Lion-Heart', was himself a *trouvère*. He wrote this song when he was captured on his way home from the Crusades. There is an interesting legend that when Richard was secretly imprisoned again later on, his minstrel Blondel travelled from castle to castle, singing this song wherever he went. At last he heard Richard's voice, joining in the song, floating up from a dungeon. Blondel was then able to secure the King's release.

The design of the song is very simple. There are two phrases only, the first of which is repeated with different words.

1. Ka - len - da ma - ya Ni fuelhs de fa - ya Ni chanz d'au - zelh Ni flors de gla - ya
2. Non es que'm pla - ya, Pros dom - na gua - ya, Tro qu'un y - snelh Mes - sa - tgier a - ya

3. Del vos - tre belh Cors qu'em re - tra - ya 5. E ja -
4. Pla - zer no velh Qu'a - mors m'a - tra - ya, 6. E cha -

ya E'm tra - ya Na vos dom - na ve - ra - ya.
ya de pla - ya 'Lge - los ans que'm n'es - tra - ya.

1. Ja nun hons pris ne di - ra sa rai - son A - droi - te - ment, se do - lan - te - ment non.
2. Mais par ef - fort puet il fai - re chan - çon Mout ai a - mis, mais po - vre sunt li don.

3. Hon - te j a - vront, se por ma re - an - çon Sui ça deus y - vers pris.

King Richard the Lion-Heart in prison

3. Sumer Is Icumen In: a canon, or round

You probably know plenty of 'canons' or 'rounds', like *Frère Jacques* or *London's Burning*. Here is a medieval one. It was found in a manuscript at Reading Abbey, which also included a calendar. The last event recorded in the calendar was the death of the Abbot in 1238 — so we can guess that the music is from about the same time.

This canon is the earliest known music for six voices. In fact it contains *two* canons — the first for four voices, the second for two — both going on at the same time. It sounds complicated, and perhaps they thought so too in the 13th century as there are careful instructions (in Latin) on how to sing it. Here they are:

'Now it is sung thus: the others keeping silent, one begins, and when he arrives at the note after the cross, another begins, and so on with the rest.'

And all the time that this is going on, two bass voices are busily singing the shorter second canon, which is marked *Pes* (= foot). And it all fits together!

Su - mer is i - cu - men in, Llu - de sing cuc - cu, Gro - weth sed and blo - weth med, And springth the w - de nu; sing cuc - cu; A - we ble - teth af - ter lamb, Llouth af - ter cal - ve cu; Bul - loc ster - teth, bu - cke ver - teth, Mu - rie sing cuc - cu. Cuc - cu, cuc - cu, Wel sin - ges thu cuc - cu, Ne swik thu na - ver nu.

Pes: Sing cuc - cu nu sing cuc - cu.

The original medieval manuscript of *Sumer Is Icumen In*

Both the poem, which is written in Wessex dialect, and the lilting melody, perfectly match the mood of early summer.

4. *A dance from the 13th century: Estampie (Ductia)*

All dances of the 13th and 14th centuries were of one kind, called the *estampie*. We do not know the steps for these dances, but they were most likely 'round dances', with the dancers holding hands and circling round a fountain, a tree, or even a person standing in the middle.

This dance has two instrumental parts, and is four sections long. The lower melody of the first two sections is later written five notes higher to become the upper part for sections 3 and 4. It is not known which instruments would have played the dance, but there would have been brightly contrasted strands of sound, and colourful percussion instruments to accent the lively dance-rhythm. This *estampie* was found in the same manuscript as 'Sumer Is Icumen In'.

5. 'Tristan's Lament' and 'La Rotta': a pair of dances from the 14th century

Tristan (sometimes called Tristram) was a Knight of King Arthur's Round Table. He came from Lyonesse, an island lying off the coast of Cornwall. Some people think that Lyonesse has long since sunk beneath the sea, but others believe it was the old name for the Isles of Scilly.

Tristan journeyed to Ireland to bring the Princess Iseult to Cornwall to marry his uncle, King Mark. But during the voyage, both drank unknowingly of a love potion and immediately fell in love with each other.

Tristan's Lament is a slow, rather melancholy dance in three-time, followed by a more lively, cheerful dance with two beats to a bar, called *La Rotta*. The first section of each dance is shown on this page. If you listen carefully, you will hear that *La Rotta* uses snatches of melody from the slower *Lament*.

The kind of ceremony at which Tristan was made a knight

6. 'Make We Joy Now in This Fest': a carol from the 15th century

One of the most popular kinds of music in the 15th century — particularly in England — was the *carol*. Carols were written for various occasions, but especially, of course, for Easter and Christmas. The verses were sung by one singer, or a small group of singers, alternating with the *burden* (or refrain) which was sung by everyone. *Make We Joy Now in This Fest* is partly in English, partly in Latin. The lively rhythm reminds us that carols were originally danced as well as sung.

25

Elizabethan Music-making

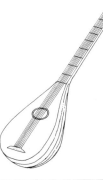

Viols

Viols had sloping shoulders (like the modern double bass) and flat backs. They had six strings, and the fingerboard was fretted (like a guitar) with pieces of gut, showing where to place the fingers to obtain the different notes. The viol was held downwards in front of the player — more like a cello than a violin. The tone was softer, more 'reedy' than that of modern string instruments.

Music was a very important part of life in Elizabethan England. It was a time when England was described as 'a neste of syngynge byrdes' (a nest of singing birds). Interest in music was so keen that almost everyone could read music at sight. Often, when supper was cleared away, a madrigal book would be placed in the middle of the table, the words and music set out in such a way that each singer had his part facing him.

Most households possessed recorders and viols in various sizes. A family of such instruments was called a *chest,* since that was how they were stored. A group of Elizabethan instruments playing together was known as a *consort.* If the instruments were all from the same family — viols, for instance, or recorders — it was called a *whole consort.* But if there was a mixture of different types of instruments — such as viols, recorders and lutes — then it was known as a *broken consort.*

Dances at court or in large houses, and pieces of music for outdoor occasions, were often played by instrumental groups so large and varied that they could be called a *band.* These included shawms (ancestors of the oboe), sackbuts (an early kind of trombone), cornetts (curved, wooden instruments with a trumpet-like mouthpiece), and percussion.

The lute

The lute was a plucked string instrument shaped like half a pear. The fingerboard was fretted, and the peg-box was bent back at an angle. There were usually eleven strings. Lutes were made in various sizes. They were very popular, either as a solo instrument, as a member of a group, or as an accompaniment to singing. A lute was often to be found hanging in a barber's shop to amuse waiting customers.

The virginals

The most popular keyboard instrument in Elizabethan households was the virginals. This was really a simple type of harpsichord. When a key was pressed down, a piece of wood called a *jack* rose up inside and plucked the string with a plectrum made of quill or leather. The notes quickly died away, but by using ornaments (a trill on a long note, for example) composers managed to create the illusion of sustained sound.

The strings of the virginals ran parallel to the keyboard. Sometimes the instruments were supplied with legs, but were often a mere box to be placed on a table. Elizabeth I was fond of playing the virginals. A visiting ambassador once reported: 'The Queene plaied quite well upon the virginals — that is, for a queene . . . '

The virginals which may once have belonged to Queen Elizabeth I. Her coat of arms is to the left of the keyboard

Madrigals

In 1558, the same year as the Spanish Armada, a book of Italian madrigals with English words was published in England. This book caused such great interest that English composers soon began to write madrigals themselves.

Madrigals were usually composed for four or five voices, each voice with its own independent rhythm and an interesting melodic line to sing. Composers made great use of *imitation* — a snatch of melody in one voice would immediately be imitated by the same snatch of melody in another voice. And there was great deal of *word-painting*. The word 'death', for instance, might be expressed in the music by a harsh chord; a phrase like 'one by one came tripping down' might have the voices, one by one, running lightly down a scale, and so on.

A sixteenth century picture, showing various aspects of music, called *The Personification of Music*

All Creatures Now Are Merry-Minded: a madrigal, by John Bennet

In 1601, the composer Thomas Morley published a collection of madrigals by various composers, called *The Triumphs of Oriana*. These madrigals, each ending with the same two lines of words, were written in honour of Elizabeth I, sometimes called 'Oriana' in poetry. *All Creatures Now Are Merry-Minded* comes from this collection.

There is some vivid *word-painting*. Listen to the gay and lively way in which Bennet treats such words as *'merry*-minded' and 'fa-la-laing'. At the words 'yond *bugle* was well winded' the voices really sound like bugles, and seem to flutter smoothly in mid-air at 'birds over her do *hover'*. Listen also for *imitation* between the voices — especially at 'the shepherds' daughters playing'.

All creatures now are merry-minded.
The shepherds' daughters playing,
The nymphs are fa-la-laing,
Yond bugle was well winded.
At Oriana's presence each thing smileth.
The flowers themselves discover;
Birds over her do hover;
Music the time beguileth.
See where she comes with flowery garlands crowned.
Queen of all queens renowned.
Then sang the shepherds and nymphs of Diana:
Long live fair Oriana.

Now is the Month of Maying: ballett, by Thomas Morley

A *ballett* was a lighter kind of madrigal copied from the Italian *balletto,* which was originally danced as well as sung. So an Elizabethan *ballett* has a lively, dance-like rhythm. There were two or more verses, all set to the same music, and always with a refrain in which the voices sang 'fa-la-la'.

'Now is the Month of Maying' has three verses (the first is printed below). In the third verse, 'shall we play barley-break?' refers to an Elizabethan version of the game of hide-and-seek.

Now is the month of Maying,
When merry lads are playing,
Fa-la-la.

Each with his bonny lass,
Upon the greeny grass,
Fa-la-la.

Ayres, or songs

There was a third kind of madrigal, called an *ayre* (song). Ayres were often printed on two facing pages, with the upper part on the left page and the lower parts on the right. Beneath the upper part was an arrangement of the lower parts which could be played on a lute. This meant that the ayre might be performed in any one of three ways: by a single voice with lute accompaniment; by a single voice accompanied by other instruments, such as viols; or by unaccompanied voices. In performance, singers and instrumentalists were able to share the same book.

'Come Again, Sweet Love'; and 'Fine Knacks for Ladies': ayres, by John Dowland

One of the most famous composers of ayres was John Dowland. He was the greatest lute-player of his time, and during his lifetime visited many courts throughout Europe. Many of his ayres are about the melancholy side of love. 'Come again, sweet love doth now invite' is written in a very simple style, with words and music perfectly matched. In the second half, the melody climbs higher and higher, eventually coming to rest on the word 'die'.

'Fine Knacks for Ladies' is more light-hearted, and has an attractive rhythm — especially at the end of the first phrase where an accent falls on a weak beat. The pedlar at the country fair protests: 'Though all my wares be trash, the heart is true . . .'

Consort Music

Lavolta: dance for Broken Consort from 'First Booke of Consort Lessons' (1599) by Thomas Morley

This collection of pieces is important because it was the first of its kind to state clearly exactly which instruments are to play the music. Morley's *broken consort* consists of plucked strings (lutes), bowed strings (treble and bass viol) and woodwind (recorder).

The *lavolta* was an energetic dance with three beats to a bar, slightly quicker than the *galliard* (see page 29). It was one of the first dances in which the dancers actually held each other. There were swift leaps and turns, and at certain points the gentleman was required to swing his partner high into the air. Queen Elizabeth much enjoyed this dance — but at the French court it was banned, as it was too unseemly!

Morley's 'Lavolta' contains only two tunes, played in this order:

$$\| : A : \| : B : \| : A : \| : B : \|$$

Morley makes his music more interesting by writing *divisions,* or varied repeats, of each tune.

Keyboard Music

The Earle of Salisbury: pavan with galliard, by William Byrd

Elizabethan composers soon discovered a style well suited to the keyboard — intricate decorations, spread chords, and brilliant running passages. In 1611, 'the first musicke that ever was printed for the Virginalls' was brought out with the title *Parthenia*. This contained 21 pieces by William Byrd, John Bull and Orlando Gibbons (born at intervals twenty years apart: 1543, 1563 and 1583).

These two dances, which Byrd dedicated to the Earl of Salisbury, Queen Elizabeth's Secretary of State, are contrasted in mood and rhythm. A *pavan* was a slowish, stately dance with two beats to a bar; a *galliard* was in three-time with quicker, more elaborate steps.

Byrd's Pavan (**A**) is in two sections — each eight bars long, and each repeated. In bars 5-7 a phrase in the right hand is imitated by the left, giving the music a smooth sense of flow.

The Galliard also has two sections, each repeated. The theme is first heard in the left hand, soon imitated by the right. Later, a rising phrase is similarly passed to and fro between the hands.

Another Pavan and Galliard for the Earl of Salisbury, by Orlando Gibbons, is included in *Parthenia*. The music is more elaborate than Byrd's, rather richer and more intense.

Queen Elizabeth I, who was fond of music and dance

'The King's Hunt': variations, by John Bull

Since printed music was scarce, collections of keyboard pieces were often copied out by hand. The largest collection we know is the 'Fitzwilliam Virginal Book', named after its last private owner. But it should really be called 'Francis Tregian's Virginal Book', for that is the name of the man who actually copied the music into the book. Tregian was a Cornishman who was imprisoned because of his religious beliefs from 1609 until his death in 1619. Many of the 297 pieces must have been copied when he was kept in the Fleet Prison in London.

'The King's Hunt' comes from this collection. Bull's variations (**B**) vividly describe the atmosphere of the hunt — galloping hooves, hunting calls and jingling harnesses. The music gradually becomes more intricate as Bull introduces more decorations, repeated notes and swift running passages for both hands.

'The Fall of the Leafe': by Martin Peerson

To make a short piece more interesting, Elizabethan composers would often write a decorated *variation* after each section. 'The Fall of the Leafe' is a quiet piece, expressing the gentle melancholy of autumn. There are two sections, each followed by its own variation. Here is the first phrase, (**C**) and the beginning of its variation (**D**):

29

Peter Warlock ENGLAND 1894-1930

Capriol Suite

Peter Warlock

Peter Warlock's real name was Philip Heseltine. He was both a writer and a composer. As a writer about music and as editor of a music magazine called *The Sackbut,* he used his own name. As a composer, he used the name Warlock — which is an old name for a male witch or wizard. He made friends with the English composer, Delius, who gave him advice about composing music and influenced him a great deal. Warlock became very interested in Elizabethan music and wrote about a hundred songs, many of them to Elizabethan words. But he only wrote three pieces for orchestra, one of them a serenade for strings in honour of Delius's 60th birthday. It is a lilting, flowing piece, capturing a great deal of the serene mood of Delius's own music. Later in life, Warlock suffered many tensions, and in the end committed suicide.

Warlock took six dance tunes from an old book entitled *Orchésographie* (the study of dancing) and arranged them for string orchestra. The book was written by a French priest, Jehan Tabourot, in the 16th century. He too used a pen-name. By re-arranging the letters of his name he called himself Thoinot Arbeau. The rhythms and steps of popular 16th century dances are discussed by Arbeau and a lawyer named Capriol — that's why Warlock calls his music *The Capriol Suite.* (The drawings at the top of the page are taken from *Orchésographie* by Arbeau.)

1. Basse-danse

In this dance the feet glided along, barely leaving the ground — hence the name *basse-danse* ('low-dance') compared with other dances which included skips, kicks or leaps.

The tune **(A)** is shared between first and second violins. At bar 12, Warlock adds a little spice to the harmony: beneath the C sharp of the violins, the cellos play C natural. Notice, too, how he gives the rhythm a 'modern' flavour by using *syncopation* — sometimes placing a strong chord on a weak beat.

2. Pavane

This gracious, stately dance often began an evening of dancing. The couples advanced in a slow, majestic procession. It used to be said that the *pavane* took its name from the Latin word *pavo,* meaning 'peacock', and this does seem to match the idea of ladies in colourful, flowing dresses, proudly strutting beside their partners. But it is now thought to come from the Italian word *padovana* (from the town of Padua).

The rhythm of the dance was often played on a kind of drum called a *tabor.* Warlock asks the violas to play this rhythm while the first violins take the beautiful melody **(B)** — two 8-bar phrases, each repeated. Then it is all played again, but this time with cellos singing

the flowing melody while high violins and violas play a 'descant', and double basses take over the tabor-rhythm.

3. Tordion

At one time, the *basse-danse* was in three parts, the third one called *tordion*. Warlock's arrangement is rhythmic and delicate. At no point do the sounds rise above *mf* (half-loud). The music is marked 'very lightly' and played *staccato* — crisp and detached **(C)**.

The second half of the piece is played *pizzicato* (plucked) and is a variation of the first. But instead of sounding more complicated, as variations often do, the reverse happens. Unimportant notes are stripped away, so the texture becomes lighter still. The music rises higher . . . then descends for two rhythmic bars marked *pppp*.

4. Bransles

The *bransle* or *branle* (from French: *branler* 'to swing') was once a lively country dance, performed in a circle with a sideways step. Later, it became popular at court. In England it was sometimes called a *brawl*. In his diary, Pepys describes Charles II dancing the Bransle:

'. . . *and the King in his rich vest of some rich silk and silver trimming, as the Duke of York and all the dancers were, some of cloth of silver, and others of other sorts, exceeding rich. Presently after the King was come in, he took the Queene, and about fourteen more couple there was, and begun the Bransle.*'

Warlock's dance is in three sections. The first is in G minor and, like the Tordion, is played softly and 'very lightly' **(D)**.

The middle section is in G major, and contrasts *staccato* bowing with *legato* (smooth). Then the first tune returns, in G minor again, and the music grows gradually louder and faster. Later on it is marked 'still faster', and ends very excitingly, *fff*.

5. Pieds-en-l'air

The title means 'feet in the air'. The music flows gently along, the serene melody played throughout by the first violins **(E)**. The melody is played through again with changed harmonies. It floats gently upwards in the final bars, marked 'much slower'.

6. Mattachins

This was a Sword Dance performed by men in 'armour' of silvered or gilded cardboard. The music is vigorous. Violins take the tune **(F)** while cellos play the same rhythm (but brisker) as the tabor rhythm of the Pavane.

Although this is a very old tune, Warlock writes harmonies which are definitely of the 20th century. The exciting clashes towards the end suggest the rhythmic clashing of the dancers' swords.

In his book, Arbeau gives this good advice to dancers:
'*When you dance in public, never look down to examine your steps to see if you are dancing correctly. Hold your head and your body upright, look confident — and do not spit or blow your nose too much . . .*'

Maurice Ravel FRANCE 1875-1937

BOLERO

Ravel was born in a small village called Ciboure, near the Spanish border in the region of the south of France known as the Basque country. When he was 12, his family moved to Paris, but all his life Ravel thought of Ciboure as 'home', and vividly remembered the Spanish folk-tunes he had heard there as a boy. In fact, several of his pieces have associations with Spain — the *Spanish Rhapsody* for orchestra, the rhythmic, sparkling *Alborada del Gracioso* (which means 'The Jester's Morning-Song'), and the haunting 'Pavane for a Dead Infanta' (an *Infanta* is a Spanish princess).

When, in 1928, the famous dancer Ida Rubenstein asked Ravel to write a piece for her, he decided to write more music with a Spanish flavour. He wrote a fifteen-minute piece for orchestra, using a melody of his own and called this music *Bolero*. (A *bolero* is a Spanish dance in which the rhythm is usually accented by castanets.) From the beginning to the end of the piece the snare-drum beats out this rhythm:

Above this insistent rhythm, a long winding melody in two sections (**A** and **B**, below) is repeated over and over again — but always with different *orchestration*.

The snare-drum (or side-drum)
This drum was originally used in the army. It was carried slung to the *side* so the player could still march along. It has two drumheads. The lower one has lengths of catgut or wire stretched across it, called *snares*. When the player hits the upper skin (usually with hard-headed sticks) the snares vibrate against the lower skin, making a dry, rattling sound.

This music has sometimes been described as monotonous — but the never-ceasing rhythm on the snare-drum, by its very repetitiveness, becomes 'hypnotic', and builds up terrific tension in the listener. (The same effect has often been experienced by people listening to African drumming.) The tension is further increased by the fact that there is a gradual *crescendo* throughout the music — more and more instruments join in until, eventually, the entire orchestra is playing.

This is how Ravel orchestrates and builds up his music:

1. A snare-drum, supported by *pizzicato* violas and cellos, beats out a soft, crisp rhythm, which will continue in a gradual fifteen-minute *crescendo*. The first part of the melody **(A)** is heard in the lower register of the flute.

2. This part of the melody is repeated by clarinet.

3. The second part of the melody **(B)** is played by a bassoon.

4. Then this is repeated by the high-pitched E flat clarinet.

5. **(A)** Played by an *oboe d'amore* (lower than an ordinary oboe, softer and more mellow — which accounts for its name 'oboe of love'). The tread of the accompaniment becomes fuller as second violins and double basses join in.

6. **(A)** An interesting sound — flute combined with muted trumpet.

7. **(B)** The smooth, slinky tone of a tenor saxophone contrasts with the sharp sound of the muted trumpet which now imitates the snare-drum rhythm by repeating the note 'G'.

8. **(B)** The higher-pitched sopranino saxophone takes over.

9. **(A)** Two piccolos, horn and celesta. Ravel achieves a 'Chinese' effect: the first piccolo plays in E major, the second in G major, while horn and celesta play in C major.

10. **(A)** Oboe, oboe d'amore, cor anglais, and two clarinets take the melody, against bright 'stabs' from two muted trumpets. The string accompaniment now becomes more elaborate.

11. **(B)** A breath of the circus, as a trombone plays the melody with occasional sliding effects.

12. **(B)** From now on the melody is played by groups of instruments in various combinations. First: the bright, clean sound of high woodwinds.

13. **(A)** A complete contrast to the sounds heard so far as violins join in the melody for the first time.

14. **(A)** Two clarinets and tenor saxophone are added, and the violins are arranged into four sections.

15. **(B)** The snare-drum rhythm gains in power . . . Clarinets and saxophone drop out, and a trumpet is added instead.

16. **(B)** Trombone and soprano saxophone add their distinctive sounds. The melody is further strengthened by the rich tones of violins, violas and cellos, and the accompaniment is enlivened by bright stabbing chords from the brass.

17. Now we hear the melody played straight through without repeats.

Tension and excitement are further increased as a second snare-drum joins the first, crashing out the hypnotic rhythm with terrific force, and melodic line is dominated by the brilliant tone of four trumpets. So far, the music has remained firmly in C major. Now it moves to the key of E. This change of key releases some of the tension, but after only eight bars we return again to C major for four deafening bars, emphasised by bass-drum, cymbals and tam-tam (a large gong). There follows a single, poised, terrifying discord . . . then total collapse.

When *Bolero* was first played in Paris it was performed as a ballet with this story:

The scene is a tavern in Andalusia. A woman dances on a table — first with slow, swaying movements; then more excitedly. One by one the watching gypsies are aroused and surround the table. The dance becomes more violent until the stage is a swirling mass of bodies, and the woman is thrown from one man to another. Jealousy creeps in. Knives are drawn, and the men close in . . . but the woman is rescued by her partner.

Within weeks of its first performance, *Bolero* was being played in concerts, cinemas and restaurants all over the world. Ravel was genuinely surprised at its popularity. He wryly described the piece as 'orchestration without music'.

Ravel and the house in Ciboure (marked with a cross), where he was born

I am particularly keen there should be no misunderstanding about this piece. It was an experiment in a very special and limited direction... I have achieved what I set out to do, and it is for the listener to take it or leave it.

Alexander Porfirovich Borodin RUSSIA 1833-1887

Polovtsian Dances

from Prince Igor

Borodin was one of the group of Russian composers who called themselves 'The Five'. Besides being a composer, he was a Professor of Chemistry. His researches (resulting in several important discoveries) and daily lectures to students left him with little time to write music. He was really only able to compose at weekends, or when illness forced him to remain at home. He often used to say that when friends met him, instead of asking if he were well, they would say: 'I do hope you are ill.'

Borodin's music is full of attractive melodies. The Overture to *Prince Igor,* which includes several tunes from the opera itself, is a fine example of this. So, too, are the Polovtsian Dances from Act II. In the opera, these are sung as well as danced, but they are often played without the voice-parts.

Prince Igor occupied Borodin's thoughts for 18 years, and was still unfinished when he died. The opera was completed by his friends, Rimsky-Korsakov and Glazounov. The story is set in the 12th century, when wandering barbaric tribes from the East were fighting violently with the Russians. Igor is captured by the Polovtsi tribe, but their leader, Khan Konchak, treats his prisoner with extreme courtesy:
'I admire you, my friend. You are so fearless. I am the same! If you and I were to join forces, we could divide all Russia. We could hunt together like two tigers and satisfy our thirst with blood. Men would hear our names with terror, and accept our rule. Woe to any who would oppose us! Come, what do you say?'
(Prince Igor makes no answer. Slaves enter, followed by warriors, to entertain the prisoner with songs and dances.)

I. Dance of the Slave Girls
A quiet introduction **(A)**, shared between flute and clarinet, leads into a long, flowing melody **(B)** accompanied by spread chords on the harp. This beautiful, sad melody — beginning on the oboe, then passing to the cor anglais — expresses the slave girls' longing for their own country:

'Fly swiftly home on gentle breezes, songs of our native country, to the land where we sang in freedom before the days of our captivity . . .'
Later, the swaying, rhythmic accompaniment becomes more elaborate, as flutes and violins take up the theme.

2. Dance of the Savage Men
The savage men whirl and leap as the music grows gradually faster and wilder. The tune is first heard on the clarinet **(C)**, then is shared between piccolo and flute. Next, all the strings except double basses play the theme while a tambourine marks the rhythm. The tambourine rhythm becomes faster as violins and woodwind take the theme. From time to time we hear tune **(A)** with another scrap of tune added to it **(D)**.

3. Tartars' Dance

In this exciting dance, fierce warriors and slaves pay homage to the great Khan Konchak:

'Sing we praises to our glorious Khan!
Praise him for his valour, noble Khan!'

The dance begins with a strong rhythm on kettle-drum and bass-drum, and then the whole orchestra crashes in with the powerful theme (**E**). While bass-drum and kettle-drum pound out the first beat of each bar, brass and other percussion — snare-drum, cymbals, triangle — emphasise the barbaric atmosphere of this colourful music.

The short middle section is more flowing, and is a dance for the prisoners. When it is repeated, listen for decorative runs on piccolo and flute against glittering notes from harp, glockenspiel and triangle. Then the noisy first section is heard again. But the mood gradually becomes more subdued, and the dance ends quietly.

4. Dance of the Young Men

Lightly-bowed strings and snare-drum set a fast, urgent rhythm, soon joined by a falling phrase on *pizzicato* cello and bassoons (**F**). Spiky phrases on oboe and clarinet (**G**) hint at the main theme, which explodes suddenly at (**H**). Cymbal-clashes and flashing, darting scraps of tune reflect the agile movements of the young men as they leap high into the air.

5. General Dance

Most of the tunes heard so far now make a second appearance. First, the slave girls come forward to dance again. Violas now join the oboe in the first half of the theme (**B**), and there is a smooth counter-melody for cellos. In the second half of the theme, the cellos join in with the cor anglais. When, as before, the violins take up the melody, woodwind instruments in the background remind us of the spiky tune (**G**) from the beginning of the fourth dance.

Then the descending *pizzicato* notes (**F**) again introduce the swift-moving *Dance of the Young Men*.

Theme **C** reappears, played now by flutes, oboes and clarinets, and everyone joins in the wild dancing as the music of the second dance is played again. The pace quickens still further (*pizzicato* strings) and a wild run on the woodwind is followed by insistent repeated notes on trumpets and horns. Finally, the theme of the introduction (**A**) is transformed into a whirling, spinning *coda* to end the Dances in a blaze of barbaric colour.

35

Aram Khatchaturian ARMENIA (USSR) 1903-1978

Dances from the ballet

GAYANEH

Armenia (a Republic of the Soviet Union) lies to the south of the Caucasus Mountains. It was once a very large country, stretching from the Black Sea in the west to the Caspian Sea in the east. In fact, one of the earliest civilisations of the world, the Hittite civilisation mentioned in the Bible, grew up in this region. Many people believe that Noak's Ark came to rest on Mount Ararat (in Armenia) after the Flood. The Armenians have a language and alphabet of their own and an extremely rich heritage of folk music.

Sabre Dance

This vivid music perfectly matches its title. An off-beat rhythm on the snare-drum introduces a tune coloured mainly by the xylophone (**A**). Each phrase is answered by 'sneers' from the muted brass. The smooth, rich tone of a saxophone takes the contrasting melody (**B**), and the insistent off-beat rhythm passes to the tambourine. When the saxophone repeats this melody, the flute adds bird-like decorations. Then the snare-drum resumes its battering, as a linking passage for xylophone and blazing brass leads back to the first tune again. This time, there is an exciting, syncopated 'interruption' to the tune for brass and suspended cymbal, struck with a drum-stick.

xylophone

muted trumpet
snare-drum

Khatchaturian was the son of a poor Armenian book-binder. He showed little interest in music until the age of nineteen, when he went to live with his brother in Moscow. It was then that he decided to become a composer.

His music is powerful, full of dramatic contrasts, and the orchestral writing is always imaginative and colourful. Sometimes Khatchaturian uses the melodies and dance-rhythms of his native country. More often, the music is of his own invention, yet strongly flavoured by the colourful characteristics of Armenian folk music.

The ballet *Gayaneh* is set on a collective farm in Armenia. The lovely Gayaneh is a cotton-picker on the farm. The ballet tells of the love and tragedy in her life, and of the cruel treatment she receives from her husband, Giko, a brutal drunkard.

Awakening and Dance of Ayshe

Beneath a haze of high, fluttering violins, double basses begin a slow swaying rhythm. Ayshe is awakened by a flute, playing in the decorative, oriental style of Armenian folk music. A rising flurry of notes from the woodwind launches into the rhythm of the dance. The lilting melody (**C**) is played several times during the dance, always by the violins but with changing orchestral colours in the background. The dance becomes livelier, and more percussion instruments are added. The calm opening mood returns, but the piece ends with loud, rhythmic chords for the full orchestra.

Lullaby

A haunting introduction for woodwind, then the flute plays a swaying melody (**D**) above a gently throbbing accompaniment. Muted violins take up the theme, and at the end of each phrase the glockenspiel plays a single note. Violins take the melody an octave higher, and now there are bright, darting figures for high woodwind and glockenspiel at the end of each phrase.

A stroke on cymbal and drums leads into the middle section, richly scored for strings. The mood gradually becomes more intense. When the first section returns, the strings present a varied treatment of the theme. The mood becomes calmer again as violas play a gently rocking rhythm and violins take the melody once more, the flute joining in the final phrases.

Lezghinka

A *lezghinka* is a wild dance of the Mahommedan tribe known as the Lezghians. This short piece is an exciting adventure in rhythm and colour. The tune (**E**) is first given to high woodwind instruments, but they are soon joined by the brass. The excitement is kept up from beginning to end by this rhythm, played on the snare-drum:

In 1954, Khatchaturian wrote another ballet called *Spartacus*. Some of the music from this has been used a great deal on television for a series called *The Onedin Line*.

I greatly admire the music of Bach, Mozart, Tchaikovsky, Borodin, Rimsky-Korsakov and Ravel. Also some of the modern works of Prokofiev and Shostakovich. But above all, I love the folk-songs of my own Armenian people.

Sir William Walton ENGLAND Born 1902

Three pieces from

Façade

William Walton

Walton is one of the great English composers of the 20th century. Like Elgar, he was mainly self-taught. Although Walton works slowly and is very self-critical, he has composed a wide variety of music. For the concert-hall he has written symphonies, concertos, an oratorio called *Belshazzar's Feast,* and several short orchestral pieces. For the Coronation of George VI in 1937 he composed a stirring march called *Crown Imperial,* and for the Coronation of Elizabeth II in 1953 he wrote another march called *Orb and Sceptre.* These are very similar in design to Elgar's *Pomp and Circumstance* Marches. Walton has also written music for many films, including Laurence Olivier's Shakespeare productions, *Henry V, Hamlet* and *Richard III.* But the very first work which brought Walton to the attention of the public was the music called *Façade,* which he wrote in 1922.

Façade was originally subtitled 'An Entertainment with poems by Edith Sitwell, for speaking-voice and six instrumentalists'. Walton wrote accompanying music to express the mood and rhythm of each poem. The first performance caused quite a stir. The musicians sat behind a curtain upon which was painted a huge mask. In order to be heard above the music, Edith Sitwell had decided to speak her poems through a megaphone fitted into the mouth of the mask. All this was considered very strange, and many people thought the poems made no sense at all. Here, though, there was some misunderstanding. Edith Sitwell explained:

THEY ARE **ABSTRACT** POEMS - THAT IS, THEY ARE PATTERNS IN SOUND.

In other words, the poems are concerned with the *sound* of words rather than their meaning, and with interesting effects achieved by rhythm and rhyme.

Later on, Walton scored eleven of the pieces for full orchestra, and some of these were eventually made into a ballet.

Swiss Yodelling Song

Walton's music conjures up the lazy atmosphere of a soft, but clear Alpine morning. A bassoon yawns its way through the melody (**A**), almost singing 'Yo-de-lay-ee-dee'! At bars 9 and 10, flute and piccolo imitate the 'sweet birds singing'. From bar 13 onwards, mention of William Tell prompts Walton to make fun of Rossini's famous Overture — while the woodwind play the shepherds' melody, a slowed-down version of the well-known galop is mournfully played by a horn, echoed by a muted trumpet, very much 'out of key'. The music ambles along, and the opening melody is heard frequently. Later on, listen for the glockenspiel imitating cowbells. At the end, there is another solemn reference to *William Tell*.

Tango-Pasodoble

In this piece Walton makes fun of a popular song of the time. After a call to attention from the snare-drum, a cor anglais in its high register turns the well-known melody, 'I do like to be beside the seaside', into a slinky tango (**B**). Then comes a rowdy, faster section in the style of an old music-hall song which sounds as if it might have rather rude words! (**C**). Much of the noise is contributed by the brass and cymbals. Then the swaying tango rhythm returns. Trumpets have the seaside tune again, and castanets add to the Spanish atmosphere suggested by Edith Sitwell's poem. A falling phrase for violin, then oboe, clarinet, and horn — then the music ends as it began, with a sharp rap on the snare-drum.

Popular Song

Here, Walton writes a brilliant 'take-off' of the kind of dance often performed in the early part of the century in music-halls, or by concert-parties at the seaside. The music is relaxed but very rhythmic. Woodwind instruments are used a great deal as soloists, and snatches of tune on saxophone or muted trumpet conjure up the atmosphere of the period. The melody (**D**), given mainly to the cool, clear-toned flute, sounds like someone whistling in carefree mood, while snare-drum and off-beat cymbal suggest the sudden high kicks of the dancers. Later on, the music turns into a tap-dance with sharp, detached chords and raps on a wood block. Walton often follows the rhythm of the poem very closely.

Façade is one of Walton's most popular works and has earned him a great deal of money. When appearing on the television quiz programme, *Face the Music*, (for which 'Popular Song' serves as signature tune) he wryly described it as his 'bread and butter'.

Popular Song
Lily O'Grady,
Silly and shady,
Longing to be
A lazy lady,
Walked by the cupolas,
  gables in the
Lake's Georgian stables,
In a fairy tale
  like the heat intense,
And the mist in the woods
  when across the fence
The children gathering
  strawberries
Are changed by the heat
  into negresses . . .

39

Quiz 2

1. Musical chains
The last letter of each answer is the first letter of the next.

A
a) Well-known old English melody.
b) Exciting dance from the ballet *Gayaneh*.
c) Nationality of the composer of the *Capriol Suite*.
d) Orchestral plucked instrument.
e) Czech dance.
f) Nationality of the composer of the ballet, *Gayaneh*.

B
a) Title of Holst's suite.
b) Another name for snare-drum.
c) Elizabethan part-songs.
d) Earliest known canon for six voices.
e) Neither sharp, nor flat.
f) Pear-shaped Elizabethan plucked instrument.

C *(Medieval Instruments)*
a) Curved wind instrument, made of wood and bound with leather.
b) Pipe and . . .
c) Popular woodwind instruments.
d) The forerunner of the oboe.
e) Often accompanied songs.
f) Plucked string instrument.

2. Who wrote what?
Match each piece to its correct composer, then add each composer's country.

Bolero	Walton	Armenia
Prince Igor	Falla	France
Façade	Ravel	Spain
Gayaneh	Borodin	England
The Three-Cornered Hat	Khatchaturian	Russia

3. Instrumental roll-call
Can you name . . .
a) 1 instrument beginning with 'k'?
b) Another beginning with 'm'?
c) 2 instruments beginning with 'p'?
d) 3 instruments beginning with 'g'?
e) Another 3 beginning with 's'?
f) 4 instruments beginning with 'v'?
g) And 5, or more, beginning with 'c'?

4. Who's who?
These are jumbled composers:
a) ALFLA
b) RONBODI
c) GRAEL
d) ROCKLAW
e) SHTOL
f) TALWON
g) STILZ
h) RIGDOOR

5. What's the difference between:
a) a cornet . . . and a cornett?
b) a ballet . . . and a ballett?
c) a viol . . . and a viola?
d) a French horn . . . and an English horn?
And can you give two different meanings of these musical words?
e) piano f) bell g) bass h) key

6. Musical anagrams
When you have answered these questions, take the first letter of each answer. When rearranged, these letters will make another musical word.

A
a) This Elizabethan dance usually followed a Pavan.
b) Composer of *Bolero*.
c) Arbeau's famous book about dancing.
d) Elizabethan song — usually for solo voice and lute.
e) Christian name of the composer of *Capriccio Espagnol*.

B
a) Nationality of the composer of the *Polovtsian Dances*.
b) Christian name of the composer of the *Sabre Dance*.
c) Recorders and viols playing together make up a *broken* . . .
d) Woodwind instrument with a double reed.
e) Words sometimes sung to Elgar's *Pomp and Circumstance* March No. 1 in D major.

7. Odd man out
In these groups of instruments, who is the 'odd man out' and why?
a) Oboe, cor anglais, clarinet, bassoon.
b) Xylophone, tambourine, triangle, snare-drum.
c) Trumpet, horn, trombone, tuba.
d) Virginals, clavichord, harpsichord.
e) Shawm, sackbutt, cornett, lute.

8. Crack the codes
Can you discover the key to these musical sentences?
a) 'DBSNFO' JT BO PQFSB, TFU JO TQBJO, CZ UIF GSFODI DPNPPTFS CJAFU.
   (To help you, the ninth word is 'the'.)
b) SGD DKHYZADSGZM HMRSQTLDMS BZKKDC SGD UHQFHMZKR VZR Z JDXANZQC HMRSQTLDMS HM VGHBG SGD RSQHMFR VDQD OKTBJDC. (Here, 'the' is the first word.)
c) HRWV WIFN RH ZMLGSVI MZNV ULI HMZIV WIFN (No help here!)

40

Johannes Brahms GERMANY 1833-1897

Hungarian Dances Nos.1 and 5

flute

triangle

violin

Brahms was the son of a double bass player. His father was keen that the boy should also become a musician and so he was taught to play the violin, cello, horn and piano. Soon he was playing piano accompaniments for his father at dances and in local taverns, where the wages were 'Twee Daler un' Duhn' (two talers and free brandy). Before he was fourteen, Brahms was pianist at a tavern in the dock area of Hamburg. And all this time he was composing music whenever he could. His piano-teacher believed that he might become a great pianist — 'if only he would stop that composing!' — but writing music was to become his whole life.

By the time Brahms was seventeen, he was giving solo performances at concerts, and also acting as accompanist to other musicians. It was at this time that he met a Hungarian violinist called Remenyi, who was half gypsy. The two of them visited Hungary, giving concerts together, and this was how Brahms was introduced to Hungarian gypsy music. He often brought touches of it into his own music — for example, the finale of his Violin Concerto.

Brahms arranged some of the gypsy tunes he had heard for piano duet, offering them to his publisher as 'genuine gypsy children'. Later on they were arranged for full orchestra. The dances are colourful and exciting. There are frequent pauses and abrupt changes of pace and mood, varying from a wistful sadness to sudden outbursts of fiery abandon.

Hungarian Dance No.1

Violins, low and rich in tone, play a rather wistful melody (A). At the end of each phrase there is a sparkling descending figure for high woodwind and triangle. The scurrying second theme (B) is in contrast to the first. In the middle section of the dance the music suddenly becomes slower and heavier (C) and there are contrasts, too, between *forte* and *piano*. Then the first part of the dance is played again.

Hungarian Dance No. 5

The contrasts in this dance are sharper still. The first melody is fiery and gay, but with an undercurrent of sadness (D). It begins in the low, rich register of the violins; but soon climbs higher, then scurries down again. During the second theme (E) there is a pause, followed by a quiet, wistful phrase; then a sudden return to high spirits. The faster middle section plunges into the bright key of F sharp major (tune F), and there are more abrupt changes of pace and mood: two slow bars with a crescendo on each note, followed by two quicker bars. Then the opening melody returns and the first part of the dance is heard again.

Both these dances are in *ternary* design: the same music at the beginning and the end, but with contrasting material in the middle — a kind of 'musical sandwich' in fact.

41

Antonin Dvořák CZECHOSLOVAKIA (BOHEMIA)
1841-1904

SLAVONIC DANCES Nos. 1, 3 AND 8

Dvořák was born in a tiny village on the banks of the River Vltava. His father who was both the butcher and the village innkeeper, loved music and often entertained customers with a song, or a tune on the zither or the violin, so it was natural that his son should also take an interest in music. At sixteen, Dvořák was sent to Prague, the capital city, to study music seriously. He later became a viola-player in the orchestra of the newly built National Theatre, where the conductor was the famous Czech composer Smetana.

Dvořák visited England several times. Here is part of a letter written by him in English. He asks that in future all letters be written to him in English also.

Dvořák eventually married and settled down to a simple, contented way of life. He loved his family, and was quite happy to compose music in the kitchen where the noises, instead of distracting him, seemed only to deepen his concentration. Besides music, he had other interests. He was very fond of gardening, and kept a large flock of pigeons. He also had a passion for trains! He would often stroll down to the railway lines, noting down the numbers of the huge engines which passed by.

When Brahms heard some of Dvořák's music he was very impressed. He sent some songs which Dvořák had written to his own publisher, Simrock. They were printed and proved to be so popular that Simrock asked Dvořák to compose 'a set of dances in Slavonic style, similar to the Hungarian Dances of Herr Brahms which are selling so favourably'. Dvořák eagerly accepted the invitation and set to work.

Like Brahms, Dvořák wrote his dances first for piano duet, scoring them for orchestra later on. But whereas Brahms had merely arranged exisiting gypsy tunes; Dvořák's melodies were all of his own invention. They were, however, very much in the *style* of folk melodies, and he used the rhythms of actual folk dances. Major and minor keys alternate, and when a melody is repeated, Dvořák usually treats it in a new and interesting way. These dances made Dvořák famous throughout Europe.

Slavonic Dance No. 1 in C major: Furiant

A *furiant* is a Czech 'swagger-dance', with a great deal of syncopation. The spirited first theme **(A),** with loudly clashing cymbals, is written with three fast beats to each bar, but the accents on the weak second beat of alternate bars make the music sound as if it has three medium-paced beats to a bar. As you listen, try counting in threes. You will find that when tune **B** arrives you will still be counting three — but twice as fast.

The tune of the contrasting middle section is crisply played by the woodwind **(C).** Dvořák gives the cellos a smooth counter-melody to play at the same time. The first part of the dance is played again, then the music becomes slower. There are reminders of scraps of tunes **B** and **C** — then the dance ends with the first theme, the cymbals clashing as furiously as ever.

Slavonic Dance No. 3 in A flat major: Polka

The *polka* is a Czech dance with 2 beats to a bar. It comes from the Czech word *pulka,* meaning 'half', and the story goes that it was invented by a Bohemian servant-girl who was forced to take very short dance steps because of the smallness of her room.

The main theme is graceful and flowing, with a smooth line for the cellos **(D).** When it is repeated later, the violins add a 'wavy' decoration. Then, an abrupt contrast — a fiery tune beginning with three strongly-punched chords **(E).**

The middle section has a lilting melody **(F),** and again the cellos have a smooth counter-melody to play. Later, the cellos themselves play the melody while the violins play a delicate line high above. Tune **E** bursts in again, followed by the first graceful theme played by the woodwind. Then tune **E** once more, growing faster and faster to end the dance in a breathless whirl of excitement.

Slavonic Dance No. 8 in G minor: Furiant

The first tune is syncopated in typical *furiant* style — two bars where the accents fall strongly into two-beat groups, followed by two normal bars of three beats each **(G).** The first half of this tune is in G minor, the second half in G major. The central section of the dance has a *legato* (smooth) melody for flute and oboe above *staccato* (crisp) string chords **(H).**

Notice the strong contrasts used by Dvořák in this dance —

between: *major* and *minor; f* and *p; staccato* and *legato.* There are contrasts, too, of mood (the quick, fiery first theme and the smooth, flowing central melody); and of orchestration — the way in which Dvořák selects and combines his orchestral colours.

George Frederick Handel GERMANY (later settled in ENGLAND) 1685-1759

MUSIC FOR THE ROYAL FIREWORKS

George Frideric Handel

In 1748, a peace treaty was signed to bring an end — for the time being, at any rate — to the wars between France and England. Early in the following year, George II decided to celebrate this event with a magnificent firework display in Green Park in London, and asked Handel to compose music for it. A huge wooden building was put up in the Park, with an enormous gallery for the musicians. Above the building was a vast sun which was to burst into flames during the display.

A few days before the event, Handel rehearsed his music in Vauxhall Gardens. In those days Handel was a popular figure in London. The rehearsal attracted twelve thousand people and the traffic on London Bridge was held up for three hours. And everyone willingly paid half-a-crown, an enormous sum in those days — merely to attend the rehearsal.

On the night itself, 101 brass cannon fired a royal salute to start the proceedings, and Handel began to conduct his music. Unfortunately, the fireworks themselves were disappointing. Some went off in fits and starts; others merely fizzled and went out. Only the enormous sun blazed gloriously on high, 'lighting the Park as if it were day'. The crowd became impatient. Then came an unexpected climax — the huge wooden building caught fire! People began to panic, pushing and jostling, so that many fell to the ground and were trodden underfoot.

But in spite of everything Handel's music was a great success. As it was for outdoor performance he chose only wind and percussion instruments. It has been said that his orchestra consisted of 24 oboes, 12 bassoons, double bassoons, 9 trumpets, 9 horns, 3 pairs of kettle-drums, and side-drums. Later on, for indoor performances, Handel reduced the number of players, and also added parts for string instruments.

Bourrée

A fast, light-footed dance for strings, oboes and bassoons only. This, like all the remaining pieces in the suite, is in *binary* design, that is, in *two* clear sections, with each section repeated. Then Handel asks that the whole piece be played through again, this time by strings only **(A)**.

44

Siciliano: La Paix

The title means 'Peace'. It is thought that this music was played during the illumination of a figure of Peace, attended by Neptune, God of the Sea, and Mars, the God of War. A *siciliano* is a flowing dance with a swaying rhythm, probably originating from the island of Sicily. Handel uses all his intruments except drums. Violins, trumpets and oboes play the melody **(B)**, occasionally joined by the horns.

Allegro: La Réjouissance

This lively piece expresses the general rejoicing of the British people at the signing of the Peace Treaty with France. It is first played by trumpets, drums and strings **(C)**. Then Handel directs that it should all be played twice more: 'The second time by the French Horns and Hautbois and Bassoons without Trumpets. The third time all together.'

Minuets I and II

The *Music for the Royal Fireworks* ends with two contrasting minuets. The first is graceful, scored for strings and woodwind only **(D)** and is played twice. The second minuet is more sturdy **(E)** and is played three times: first by trumpets, woodwind, strings and kettle-drums;

then by hunting horns with oboes, bassoons and kettle-drums; and finally by everyone together, including the side-drums, so making an impressive ending to the suite. Even though the fireworks were mainly unsuccessful, Handel's music considerably made up for the disappointment.

Original letter
written by Handel

Eighteenth century picture of the fire at the royal firework display

Giuseppe Tartini ITALY 1692-1770

Violin Sonata in G Minor "The Devil's Trill"

The violin
Making a violin demands great skill and knowledge. Each instrument has more than 70 parts. Some of the finest violins were made in Cremona, Italy, in the 17th and early 18th centuries by the Amati and Guarneri families, and — the finest craftsmen of all — Stradivarius. There are more than a thousand of his violins still being played all over the world.

One night, during his stay in the monastery at Assisi, Tartini had a strange dream.

'One night I dreamed I had made a bargain with the Devil for my soul. Then, the idea came to me of handing him my violin to see what he would make of it. Great was my astonishment when I heard him play, with the greatest skill, a Sonata of such exquisite beauty that it far surpassed the boldest flights of my imagination. I was enraptured . . . My breath failed me, and — I awoke. Seizing my violin, I tried to reproduce the sounds I had heard. But in vain. The piece I then composed, The Devil's Trill, *although the best I ever wrote, was far inferior to the haunting music I had heard in my dream.'*

Tartini's father was a wealthy Italian nobleman who lived in the town of Padua. He often gave large sums of money to the Church, and hoped that one day his son would become a priest. But Giuseppe was far more interested in fencing and music — in fact, be became so skilled as a fencer that he was soon able to defeat anyone who dared to challenge him.

When he was 20, Tartini secretly married the niece of a powerful Cardinal called Cornaro. The marriage was soon discovered, and Tartini was forced to flee from Padua in order to escape the Cardinal's anger. He eventually arrived at Assisi, and found refuge in a monastery. He began to study music in earnest. The monks enjoyed listening to him play the violin, in the refectory while they were eating their meals, or in the church during their daily services.

On festival days, visitors were welcome to attend the services. On these occasions, too, Tartini would play his violin — but always hidden behind a curtain, for fear that someone might recognise him. The fame of the mysterious violinist and his glorious music soon spread. It was on the Feast of St. Francis as Tartini was playing his violin as usual, that one of the monks accidentally brushed against the curtain. The mysterious violinist was revealed and recognised by some visitors from Padua who had known him well.

THE DEVIL'S SONATA.

As soon as they arrived home they told their story. But the Cardinal's anger had cooled by now. He sent word to Tartini, urging him to return to Padua to be reunited with his wife. And so Tartini left the monastery and returned to Padua, eventually to become one of the greatest composers and violin teachers in Italy. He gave violin lessons to students from so many countries that his house became known as 'The School of Nations'.

Sonata is the Italian word for 'sounded'. It was first used to describe music to be *played* (as distinct from *cantata* — music to be *sung*). Later on, the word came to mean music for one or two instruments written in several *movements*.

A *trill* is a form of decoration — usually the alteration of the note written with the note immediately above. A trill indicated in the music as:

would sound as: etc.

Double stopping is a special technique which a violinist can use to make two notes sound at once; that is, the bow causes two strings to vibrate at the same time.

1. Larghetto affettuoso *(larghetto* means 'fairly slowly', *affettuoso* — 'with feeling').* The violin plays a melody with a gently swaying rhythm **(A)**. This movement is in *binary,* or two-part, design. Both sections end in a similar way — with double-stopping on the violin — so that the movement sounds balanced. There is another passage of double-stoppings just after the beginning of the second section. Here, the violin is really playing two melodies, so that it sounds almost as if *two* violins are playing at the same time.

2. Allegro *(lively).* This movement is also in binary design. It begins with a vigorous, strongly-bowed theme **(B)** which descends to the lowest note of the violin. Then follows music which is more lightly-bowed, with a lot of trills and precise decorations against an accompaniment of light, repeated chords.

3. The last movement is made up of alternating sections marked *grave* (seriously — slow and solemn) and *allegro*, boldly contrasting with each other in pace and mood.

First, the slow introduction **(C)** followed by a more lively tune with double-stoppings **(D)**. In this *allegro* section comes the first of the passages of trills which give the Sonata its name. Another *grave* section follows **(E)**. The rest of the movement consists of the alternation of themes **D** and **E**. After the third appearance of the *allegro* section **(D)** the accompaniment ceases and the violin continues alone, weaving an intricate web of double-stoppings and trills of fiendish difficulty. Then the accompaniment returns, and the Sonata ends with another brief *grave* section.

In Tartini's day, the accompaniment to a Sonata would have been played on a harpsichord, or perhaps an organ. Nowadays, it is often played on a piano.

47

The Symphony

What is a Symphony?

Many of the composers you've heard about also wrote much longer pieces for full orchestra called symphonies. The word *'symphony'* actually means a 'sounding together', that is, a lot of instruments sounding together. A symphony is really a kind of 'sonata' for orchestra.

Most symphonies are made up of four separate pieces called *movements,* each one different in character. The movements are often set out in the following way.

First Movement: at a fast pace. Written in what is known as *Sonata form* — that is, three main sections which are described below.

Second Movement: at a slow pace. Perhaps in *ternary* (three-part) design; or *theme and variations;* or even *Sonata form* again.

Third Movement: Mozart and Haydn wrote a *Minuet and Trio* at this point. Beethoven and many later composers preferred to write a *Scherzo and Trio* at a faster pace. (*Scherzo* means 'a joke'.)

Fourth Movement (*Finale*): at a fast pace. *Rondo;* or *Sonata form;* or a mixture of the two. Sometimes, *theme and variations.*

Of course, this basic pattern may be varied to suit the composer's purpose. For instance, there may be a slow introduction to the first movement, or the Scherzo may come before the slow movement. The point is that the movements making up a symphony should contrast well with each other in pace and mood.

A movement in *Sonata form* has three main sections:

1. Exposition — where the composer 'exposes' or presents the tunes he is going to use. There are *two* or sometimes *three* main themes. The first theme is in the 'home' key. Then comes the *bridge passage* which leads into the second theme in a different key.

2. Development — where the composer introduces new keys, developing, or building up, his music from tunes or rhythms he has already used in the Exposition.

3. Recapitulation — where the composer 'recapitulates' or repeats in a slightly different form the music from the Exposition. The *bridge passage* has to be altered so that the second theme comes back in the 'home key'. Very often the composer adds a *coda* (Italian for 'tail') to round off the movement. The Recapitulation section balances with the Exposition since the music it uses is almost the same.

EXPOSITION			DEVELOPMENT	RECAPITULATION			CODA
FIRST THEME (in the 'home' key)	BRIDGE PASSAGE (changing key)	SECOND THEME (in a different key)	In various keys but avoiding the 'home' key	FIRST THEME (in the 'home' key)	BRIDGE PASSAGE altered to lead to:-	SECOND THEME (now also in the 'home' key)	or roundin

Wolfgang Amadeus Mozart AUSTRIA 1756-1791

First Movement from
Symphony No. 40 in G Minor

VUE DE LA VILLE CAPITALE DE   SALZBOURG AVEC LA FORTERESSE.
Dédié a l'Illustre Chapitre de   l'Eglise Metropolitaine de Salzbourg.

Wolfgang Amadeo Mozart

This is the house in Salzburg where Mozart was born

Mozart wrote 41 symphonies. His three last and greatest
symphonies (No. 39 in E flat; No. 40 in G minor and No. 41 in C,
called 'The Jupiter') are completely different from each other in mood
and character. They were all written in the summer of 1788. His wife,
Constanze, was ill, and their daughter, Theresia, had recently died.

Here is how Mozart builds up the first movement of Symphony No. 40:

Exposition

First Theme: Violas provide an accompaniment while first and second violins, an octave apart, play the first theme **(A)**, in the 'home' key of G minor. The first three notes of the theme become important later on.

Bridge Passage: Mozart begins to build up his bridge passage upon the first theme, and the music begins to leave the 'home' key of G minor to move to B flat major. Eventually, there is a more rhythmic idea **(B)**. (You will know when the end of the bridge passage is reached — there are loud chords, then a short pause.)

Second Theme (B flat major): a smoother theme **(C)**, first for strings interrupted by woodwind; then repeated, with strings and woodwind changing places. There follows a more rhythmic idea, ending with a descending scale **(D)**; then Mozart reminds us of the first theme. The Exposition section ends vigorously. (Mozart indicates that the Exposition should be repeated, but some conductors prefer to go straight on.)

Development

Mozart bases his development section entirely upon the first theme **(A)**. He embarks upon a succession of new keys, beginning in F sharp minor — a very distant key from the 'home' key of G minor. Listen for the theme to be played by the lower strings (violas, cellos and basses), echoed afterwards by the violins.

Later, the texture of the music becomes lighter as Mozart takes the idea of the beginning of the theme, giving it to strings and woodwind alternately. Then the same little three-note idea is used as a *link,* as woodwind instruments lead smoothly back to the 'home' key of G minor, and the start of the Recapitulation section.

Recapitulation

First Theme: in the 'home' key (G minor) as before.
Bridge Passage: now extended and built up, using the rhythmic tune **(B)**. The music finds its way back to the 'home' key of G minor for the second theme.

Second Theme: in the Exposition, this theme was written in B flat major **(C)**. Now it is played in G *minor,* making it sound sadder and more resigned **(E)**. The vigorous tune **(D)** follows as before, but also now in the *minor.* Again there is a reference to the main theme **(A)**.

Coda

A smooth passage for strings, as Mozart lingers a moment longer upon the main theme. Then the music ends vigorously.

Ludwig van Beethoven GERMANY 1770-1827

First Movement from Symphony No. 5 in C Minor

Beethoven had a very unhappy childhood. His father hoped that his son would make money for him by becoming a famous child pianist, as Mozart had done. He would often come home late from the tavern, very drunk, then drag the boy from his bed and force him to practise at the piano. But although Beethoven showed considerable promise as a pianist, he first came to public notice as a composer.

At 17 he went to Vienna. He played to Mozart, who remarked: 'Watch this young man, for he will make a noise in the world'. And for a short while Beethoven received lessons from Haydn. Viennese music-lovers were intrigued by Beethoven's music: it appealed to the emotions, and made an immediate impact with its strongly dramatic contrasts. In spite of his gruff manner and easily aroused temper, Beethoven made many friends, and soon publishers were eager to accept any music which he cared to show them.

In 1800 the year in which he completed his First Symphony, Beethoven recognised with horror the first signs of approaching deafness.

"If I were in any other profession perhaps it would be more bearable; but for a musician, this is the most terrible of all afflictions."

Much of his music seems to reflect his struggle to come to terms with this cruel blow which Fate had dealt him. In fact Beethoven actually said about the rhythm which is hammered out at the beginning of the Fifth Symphony: 'Thus Fate knocks at the door . . .'

As his deafness grew gradually worse, Beethoven began to avoid people. He had always loved nature, and now spent many hours walking in the countryside, always carrying a notebook into which he scribbled the musical ideas which occurred to him. Later, ideas from these untidy pages would be altered time and again before Beethoven was satisfied and ready to use them.

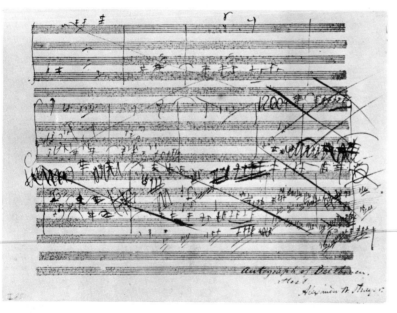

Much of the impact of the first movement of the Fifth Symphony is achieved by strong contrasts. This is how Beethoven builds up the movement:

Exposition

First theme (A): Strings and clarinets thunder out the four-note rhythm (x) which will dominate the whole movement. Then Beethoven builds up a musical paragraph upon the rhythm.

52

Bridge Passage: uses the same musical material. The full orchestra is used to build up a climax, at the end of which the music is suddenly punched into the key of E flat major.

Second Theme (B): This is dramatically introduced by rhythm x played by the horns, followed by flowing phrases first for violins, then clarinet, then violins with flute. But at the end of each phrase, the same insistent rhythm is heard menacingly in the bass. The music again builds up, the rhythm in the bass climbing higher and higher beneath flowing phrases for violins. At the height of this climax there is a *fortissimo* held chord, then angry quavers are unleashed by the violins against loud, sharply detached chords. The Exposition ends with rhythm x, pounded out by the full orchestra. (Beethoven marks the Exposition to be repeated.)

Development
Beethoven develops, or works out, his material in this way:
1. Rhythm x, punched out by wind then strings.
2. The First Theme (A), now in the key of F minor, with a smooth phrase for strings added towards the end.
3. Rhythm x, in short rising phrases for strings and woodwind in turn, leading to:
4. Crashing chords for full orchestra.
5. The first phrase of the Second Theme (B) on the violins, then the lower strings stride powerfully downwards.
6. A passage based upon bars 2 and 3 of the Second Theme: (marked y): sustained chords in dialogue between wind and strings, gradually getting softer (C).
7. There is a dramatic interruption as the first phrase of the Second Theme suddenly bursts out, *fortissimo*.
8. The mysterious dialogue between wind and strings briefly continues, only to be interrupted again — this time by rhythm x, hammered out by the entire orchestra.
   This leads the music directly into the Recapitulation section.

Recapitulation
The themes reappear in the same order as in the Exposition. But now there is a sustained line for oboe added to the First Theme, which leads into a short solo passage. And the Second Theme now appears in the key of C major.

Coda
In a movement by Haydn or Mozart, the *Coda* is usually just a 'rounding-off'. But for Beethoven, the Coda becomes a 'summing-up' as well as a conclusion. In fact, he often continues to work out his material, so that the Coda becomes a second development section. This is how Beethoven constructs the Coda to this movement:
1. First, another passage of savagely pounding chords for orchestra.
2. Then a section based upon the first phrase of the Second Theme (B), with scurrying passages for the violins, leads to:
3. what at first seems to be a new idea (D), but it is really taken from bars 6 and 7 of the Second Theme (marked z). Beethoven develops this, writing more 'dialogue' music for wind and strings.
4. Eventually, the First Theme crashes out again but now woodwind instruments 'shadow' the main notes of the melody (E).
5. Then a sequence of defiant *fortissimo* chords brings the movement to an end.

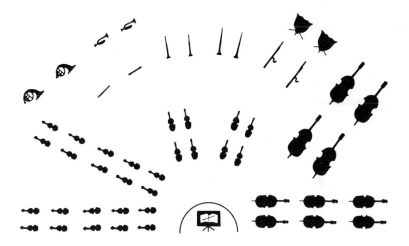

This is the kind of orchestra composers were writing for at the end of the 18th century and the beginning of the 19th: a strong section of strings, with 2 flutes, 2 oboes, 2 clarinets, 2 bassoons; 2 horns, 2 trumpets; and kettle-drums. Beethoven uses exactly these forces for the first three movements of his Fifth Symphony, but adds a piccolo, double bassoon, and 3 trombones in the finale. Compare this orchestra with the modern symphony orchestra on page 2.

Antonin Dvořák CZECHOSLOVAKIA (BOHEMIA) 1841-1904

Two Movements from
Symphony No. 9 in E Minor "From the New World"

In the summer of 1892, Dvořák arrived in America. He spent two years there as Director of the new Conservatory of Music which had been set up in New York. He was also expected to teach composition, conduct the student orchestra, and arrange concerts of his own music. At first he was fascinated by his new surroundings. Dvořák had always had two keen interests besides music: trains and pigeons. Now he found a third — the huge liners which visited New York. Whenever a famous ship was due — even if he was supposed to be at the Conservatory — he would go down to the docks to see it arrive. And he loved to be able to tell his friends in Bohemia which ship would carry his letters to them.

During his first winter in New York, Dvořák began work on his Ninth Symphony. 'It seems that America will have a good effect upon my music,' he wrote to a friend. 'I think you will be able to hear this in my new symphony.'

New York at the end of the last century

But in spite of the attractions which America offered, Dvořák soon began to miss his own country, and this feeling of homesickness was reflected in the symphony he was writing. He was persuaded to spend the summer holiday at Spillville, a town in Iowa where a large number of Czechs had settled. Among his own people for a while, Dvořák was more content. He enjoyed the peace of the surrounding countryside after the noise and bustle of New York. During his stay there he completed the orchestration of his symphony. He decided to give it a Czech title: *Z Nového Sveta,* meaning 'From the New World'.

When the symphony was performed in New York the following winter, it was a great success. Earlier, Dvořák had written a newspaper article expressing his interest in American folk music — particularly Negro Spirituals. This led some people to think that he had used existing American folk-tunes in his new symphony. Others thought the music was typically Czech in flavour, and that the title suggested a greeting from a homesick composer to his friends in Bohemia. Later, when the symphony was to be performed in

Germany, Dvořák wrote to the conductor to make his intentions clear: 'Ignore all that nonsense about my having used 'Indian' or 'American' tunes — it is untrue. I merely tried to write music in the *spirit* of actual American folk melodies'.

Each of the four movements of the symphony is full of attractive tunes. Some of the most exciting moments are when Dvořák brings back themes already heard, altering their character and presenting them in different orchestral colours.

54

Second Movement: Largo *(broadly and slowly)*

A sequence of solemn chords for the brass introduces a melody for cor anglais **(A)** which seems to express Dvořák's longing for his own country. The chords return, this time for the woodwind. After a quiet passage for strings, the cor anglais is heard again.

Snatches of the melody, played by the horns, lead into a contrasting section with two tunes: the first for flute and oboe against rustling strings **(B)**; the second for clarinets above a pizzicato bass **(C)**. Both these tunes are repeated with changed orchestration.

Now comes a brief interlude in which woodwind instruments merrily suggest birdsongs. Then the music rises to a climax, and important phrases from three different themes are combined: the trumpets play a snatch of the cor anglais melody **(A)** while, at the same time, Dvořák reminds us of two themes from the *first* movement — the main theme **(D)** on the trombones, and the third theme played by horns and violins.

The music becomes calmer, and tune **A** returns. The first part is played by the cor anglais as before, but the remainder of the melody is given to a small group of muted strings. The solemn chords for the brass are heard again. Then the strings float softly upwards, and the movement ends with mysterious chords for double basses only.

Third Movement: Molto Vivace *(very lively)*

This movement contrasts strongly in pace and mood with the previous movement. It is in the form of a *Scherzo and Trio*. There are two appearances of the *Scherzo*, the *Trio* provides contrasting music in between.

Scherzo: After a short introduction, with excitement added by triangle and kettle-drums, Dvořák builds up the first part of the Scherzo using a short, rhythmic tune **(E)**. All this music is repeated. A second tune **(F)** is played in turn by flute and oboe, clarinets, and cellos; then the first part of the Scherzo comes round again. A linking passage,

reminding us of the main theme of the first movement, leads into the Trio.

Trio: The first tune **(G)**, played by the woodwind, is rather like a Czech country dance. It is played twice. The second tune **(H)** is given to the strings, then taken over by the woodwind. Tune **G** returns, now with a dancing accompaniment for strings. Then both tunes are played once more.

The *Scherzo* section is heard again, this time leading into the *Coda* which begins with a shuddering chord for the strings. The mood darkens as the horns play the main theme from the first movement against fragments of the Scherzo theme on flute and oboe. Soon after, the trumpets play a reminder of the flute theme from the first movement. Then the music dies away.

Dmitri Shostakovich U.S.S.R. 1906-1975

First Movement from
Symphony No. 7 "The Leningrad"

During the Second World War, Shostakovich applied for service in the Soviet Army, but was told he could best serve his country by continuing to write music. In 1941 he was warned to leave Leningrad because of the danger from the advancing German army. However he stayed on and went through the Siege of Leningrad as a fire-fighter.

The U.S.S.R. (Union of Soviet Socialist Republics) covers one sixth of the land-surface of the world. As it is such a vast country, there is a very great variety of landscape and climate, from frozen wastes in the north (called *tundra*) to desert regions in the south where the climate is sub-tropical.

Only about 70% of the 212 million people of the U.S.S.R. live in what is called 'Russia'. Many different races live in the republics outside Russia proper, and more than 200 languages are spoken altogether. This makes for a rich variety of folk songs and dances, and each race is encouraged to take a pride in its own heritage. Soviet musicians are supported by the state. Composers must write the kind of music the state wants — music which can easily be understood by the people, not too 'modern' or too experimental. Several times Shostakovich has been criticised by the authorities for writing music which is too advanced — indeed, once he was condemned as a creator of noise rather than music! Even so, he became the most highly respected composer in the U.S.S.R., and one of the greatest composers of symphonies. His first symphony was written when he was only 19. It was soon played in other countries, making him known throughout the world.

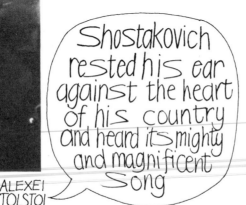

Shostakovich rested his ear against the heart of his country and heard its mighty and magnificent song

ALEXEI TOLSTOI

Taking the dead to be buried during the siege of Leningrad

56

'The city's fighting spirit was superb. Housewives, children and the aged alike bore themselves courageously. I will never forget the women of Leningrad who fought the fires and fire-bombs. They were true heroines . . . In the first hot July days, I began work on my Seventh Symphony — music inspired by thoughts of the defence of my own country. The work took all my attention. Neither the savage air-raids nor the grim atmosphere of a besieged city could hinder the flow of my musical ideas.'

In fact the first three movements were written in about two months. When the symphony was performed early in 1942, it was an immediate success. Being a symphony about war, it spoke the emotional language of the times.

Soon after the first Russian performance, the score of the symphony, on microfilm, was flown out of Russia under United Nations supervision, so that the music might be played in other countries.

'It is a *programme* composition inspired by the grim events of 1941. There are four movements. The first tells how our pleasant and peaceful life was disrupted by the forces of war. I did not intend to describe war in a realistic way (the drone of aircraft, the rumble of tanks, artillery, etc.). I wrote no so-called battle-music. I was trying to present the spirit and essence of those harsh events. The beginning of the first movement *(Allegretto)* tells of the happy life led by the people . . . the kind of life led by the Leningrad volunteer fighters before the war . . . by the entire city . . . by the entire country . . . The theme of war governs the middle passages.'
(Shostakovich writing about the Leningrad Symphony)

Points to listen for

1. A strong, heroic theme for strings (**A**). Woodwinds soon take over; then both sections combine.

2. There emerges the peaceful sound of a solo flute.

3. A more consoling theme for strings (**B**), leads to:

4. A melody for oboes (**C**). Listen for theme **B** in the bass; and, after a serene passage for strings, theme **C** high in the violins.

5. There are rich, sustained chords on the strings as a piccolo, clear and untroubled, soars high above the orchestra playing parts of themes **B** and **C**, then giving way to a solo violin.

6. This serene mood (portraying 'our pleasant and peaceful existence') is broken by a soft rhythm on the snare-drum. A march-tune is heard (**D**) which is repeated over and over with changing orchestration, but always accompanied by the snare-drum rhythm (rather as in Ravel's *Bolero*). At first, the music is almost jaunty, but it gradually grows more menacing as the tension increases. The tune is heard, in all, 12 times.

7. Then: a sudden change of key from E flat to A major. The brass rages savagely over fragments of the march-tune as the rhythm, desperate and chaotic, is pounded out by massed percussion. Sharp dissonances underline the threat of destruction. (In these passages, Shostakovich uses an extra section of trumpets, horns and trombones, set apart from the main orchestra.)

8. A climbing passage for low brass and strings leads to music completely dominated by the huge brass forces, with crashing drums, cymbals and tam-tam (gong). The heroic opening theme (**A**) is ruthlessly torn apart and hurled about the orchestra.

9. At length, the fury passes and the music comes to rest in F sharp major. A flute is heard, clear and liquid-smooth. Then a clarinet, low and rich, leads to dark-throbbing chords as a bassoon laments over themes **A** and **C**.

10. The music returns to the opening key of C major, and strings play a smooth version of theme **A**.

11. Muted brass remind us of earlier harsh rhythms — but high violins calmly reply with the consoling second theme (**B**).

12. Finally, there is an ominous reminder of the snare-drum rhythm, and we hear snatches of the march-tune on muted trumpet — a warning that the threat of war is always there.

Béla Bartók HUNGARY 1881-1945

Two Movements from Concerto for Orchestra

Bartók first became interested in folk music while he was a student at the Academy of Music. Later in life he met another Hungarian composer — Zoltán Kodály — who shared this interest. Both of them suspected that the tunes which were usually thought of as Hungarian folk music were very different from the real music of the peasants. They visited many villages — not only in Hungary, but in Rumania, Bulgaria, and other neighbouring countries as well — and between them collected more than 6,000 folk tunes which had never been written down before.

Many of these tunes had irregular rhythms. Very few were in the usual major and minor scales, and some suggested rather strange harmonies. Bartók studied them closely. He became so affected by the flavour of these folk tunes that, from then on, they influenced his own music.

Unfortunately, Bartók's compositions gained little success in his own country. In spite of many bitter disappointments, he remained in Budapest as a piano-teacher at the Academy until 1940. Then, disliking Hungary's link with Nazi Germany, he reluctantly left to settle in America. There, he achieved more success, especially when he wrote his *Concerto for Orchestra* in 1943. Bartók explained that he had called it *Concerto* because there are many instances where the orchestral instruments — either singly, or in groups — are given brilliant and difficult passages to play.

Giuoco delle Coppie: "The Game of the Couples"

This is the second of the five movements in the Concerto. It is in *ternary* design.

1. After an introduction from the snare-drum (with the snares loosened so that only the skin vibrates) we meet the 'couples' — five pairs of wind instruments accompanied by the strings. Each couple has its own special *interval* — that is, the distance between the notes played by the two instruments. First come two bassoons, playing six notes apart **(A)**; then follow two oboes playing in thirds **(B)**; two clarinets in sevenths **(C)**; two flutes in fifths **(D)**; and finally, two muted trumpets playing only two notes apart **(E)**. The snare-drum rhythm leads into the middle, contrasting section:

2. Brass instruments play a solemn *chorale,* or hymn-like melody **(F)** At the end of each phrase, the snare-drum insistently taps out its rhythm.

3. The music of the first section returns — but now the couples are joined by other wind instruments which add extra strands of colourfu sound and the string accompaniment is rather more elaborate.

snare-drum

clarinets

muted trumpets

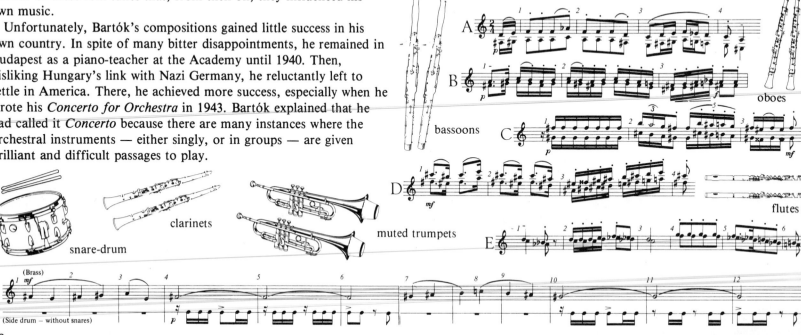

bassoons

oboes

flutes

Béla Bartók (on the right) with his friend Zoltán Kodály in Budapest

Intermezzo Interrotto: "Interrupted Intermezzo"

Intermezzo means music played 'in the middle', such as a piece played between the scenes or acts of an opera. Here Bartók writes an Intermezzo between the third and fifth movements. He described this fourth movement as **A B A — Interruption — B A.** The bar-lengths of the two main tunes **(G)** and **(H)** are constantly changing. Tune **I**, which 'interrupts', is part of a theme from Shostakovich's Seventh Symphony, which Bartók heard on the radio while working on this concerto. (Compare Tune **I** here with bars 7-10 of Tune **D** on page 57.)

A.   In this first section, woodwind instruments are the soloists, lightly accompanied by the strings **(G)**.

B.   A more flowing melody for violas, accompanied only by harps and kettle-drums **(H)**. It is repeated by the violins, with cor anglais playing the same melody but one beat later.

A.   The woodwind give a brief reminder of the music of the first section.

Interruption: the mood is broken as the pace becomes brisker and a clarinet quotes the Shostakovich theme **(I)**. Bartók evidently did not think too highly of it, for he makes the orchestra — especially the brass — greet it with loud, jeering trills and slides.

B.   Muted violins and violas calmly continue to play the flowing melody **(H)** as if nothing had happened.

A.   A reminder of the opening music, during which the strings hold a soft chord as a flute plays a short *cadenza,* or solo passage.

Igor Stravinsky RUSSIA and AMERICA 1882-1971

Suite from the ballet
The Firebird

As a student, Stravinsky learnt a great deal about orchestration from the famous Russian composer, Rimsky-Korsakov. Later, when the Russian ballet producer, Diaghilev, heard some of Stravinsky's music, he was so impressed that he asked him to write a ballet based on the Russian fairy-tale, *The Firebird*. The ballet was first performed in Paris in 1910. Its success established Stravinsky as an important composer, and encouraged him to write two more ballets for Diaghilev's company — *Petrushka,* the story of a Russian puppet, and *The Rite of Spring.*

In 1919, Stravinsky took six pieces from *The Firebird* and arranged them as a separate *suite* (or 'group' of pieces). He contrasts the rich and vivid sounds of the whole orchestra with single instruments used as soloists against a shimmering orchestral background.

The story

During a hunting expedition, Prince Ivan finds himself in an enchanted garden. A beautiful bird appears, whose dazzling feathers seem to be made of flames. Ivan captures the bird, but when she pleads to be set free, he releases her. In return, the Firebird gives him a magic feather.

The sun rises, and thirteen princesses come from the nearby castle. As they dance, they throw golden apples to each other. When they discover Ivan, they warn him that the castle and enchanted garden belong to an evil magician called King Kastchei, who captures princesses and turns young men to stone. Ivan, who has immediately fallen in love with one of the princesses, vows to enter the castle.

As he throws open the gates he sees King Kastchei and his monstrous followers. Kastchei tries to bewitch Ivan, but he is protected by the Firebird's magic feather.

The Firebird returns, and forces Kastchei and his weird band to dance until they fall to the ground exhausted. She tells Ivan of an egg which contains Kastchei's soul. Ivan smashes the egg. Kastchei dies, and the princesses are freed from his evil power.

1. Introduction

1. Bass drum, cellos and double basses set the dark, mysterious atmosphere of Kastchei's enchanted garden (**A**). Soon, there are menacing chords for the trombones (**B**).

2. Darting, rhythmic phrases for woodwind and muted trumpets alternate with Tune **A**.
3. The string players lightly brush their fingers up and down the strings, producing an eerie, slithering effect.
4. Tune **A** is played by flutes, oboe, and violins in turn.
5. The piece ends with distant horn calls, and a ripple of notes from the piano.

2. Dance of the Firebird

Although rather short, this is the most brilliant of the pieces in the suite.

1. There is a short introduction: trills on the strings change to fluttering, dancing patterns for strings and woodwind. Then short, swooping phrases lead into the dance itself.

2. The Firebird's theme is made up of glittering flashes of sound for woodwind and piano **(C)**. Later on, there are intricate rhythmic patterns for the strings, and colourful splashes of sound from the brass. Flourishes for piccolo and piano give the impression of swift, darting movements.

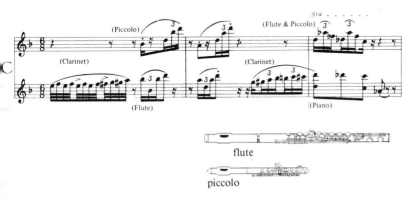

flute

piccolo

King Kastchei

3. Round Dance of the Princesses

1. Introduction: two flutes play a *canon* — that is, one flute starts to play a tune, then the second flute joins in later with the same tune **(D)**. A solo violin leads smoothly into the dance:

2. There are two tunes. The first, a Russian folk-song, begins on the oboe with harp accompaniment **(E)**, then passes to a solo cello, clarinet, and bassoon. The second tune **(F)** is for muted strings.

3. The flute *canon* returns; then both tunes are heard again, the music lingering for some time over the second tune.

4. The final bars are solos for oboe, clarinet, horn and piccolo, against a rustling background for the strings.

4. The Infernal Dance of King Kastchei

Vivid orchestral colours and syncopated rhythms mirror the twisting, darting movements of the evil magician.

1. A shrieking chord for full orchestra — and a persistent rhythm begins on the kettle-drum, played with wooden sticks. The main theme **(G)** is played by brass instruments.

2. Flute, piano and *pizzicato* violins play a variation of Tune **G**, with brilliant flashes of sound from the xylophone.

3. There are smoother phrases for violins and woodwind (**H**). Then the brass take up Tune **G** again.

4. A spiky scrap of tune for the xylophone is answered by jeering phrases for wind instruments.

5. Tune **I** is first given to the strings; then repeated by the full orchestra with thunderous chords for brass and drums.

6. The rest of the music is concerned with Tune **G**, now orchestrated even more vividly than before. Then the pace gradually increases as Kastchei leaps and whirls, bringing the dance to a breathless conclusion.

5. Lullaby

A contrast of mood and orchestration after the brilliance and excitement of Kastchei's dance.

1. Harp and violas play a soft *ostinato* — a short phrase repeated over and over again. The melody (**J**) is played by a solo bassoon.

2. A swirl of notes from the harp leads into the middle section, richly scored for the strings.

3. The bassoon melody is heard again.

4. A shadowy, shimmering passage for the strings leads without a break into the final piece.

6. Finale

Here, Stravinsky uses another Russian folk song (**K**). It is played in turn by horn; violins; strings and woodwind; and full orchestra. The music suddenly becomes softer; then with a crash on the drums, the brass play the melody. Now, the notes are of equal value, seven to each bar. Then the pace becomes twice as slow, as the melody is taken up majestically by the whole orchestra. The final triumphant chords are played by the brass against long notes for strings and woodwind.

The Firebird

Quiz 3

1. Parliamo Italiano

Make a list of all the Italian words you know, directing how music should be played. Then explain what each one means.

2. Musical Jigsaw

Clues Across

1. Low-pitched woodwind instrument.
7. Three-part design — A B A.
8. He wrote *The Three-Cornered Hat*.
9. The kind of nobleman for whom William Byrd wrote his Pavan.
10. Exciting Czech dance.
11. The number of Dvořák's *Symphony From the New World*.
12. Italian for 'plucked'.
15. Italian for 'getting louder'.
17. Essential to an organ!
18. An Elizabethan keyboard composer.
19. Stringed instrument.
20. 'The first musicke that ever was printed for the virginalls'.
21. Pear-shaped plucked instrument.

Clues Down

1. Exciting piece by Ravel.
2. Spanish for 'Spain'.
3. Rather like a trumpet.
4. A piece played *between* scenes.
5. Opera by Bizet.
6. Single-reed woodwind instrument.
10. Bizet's nationality.
12. Introductory piece of music.
13. Suite of old dances by Warlock.
14. Singing *and* acting involved here.
16. Well-known English composer.

3. Musical alphabet

1. Khatchaturian's country. A . . .
2. Russian composer — also a chemist! B . . .
3. A French opera, set in Spain. C . . .
4. Composer of *Slavonic Dances*. D . . .
5. Composer of *Pomp and Circumstance*. E . . .
6. Italian for 'very loud'. F . . .
7. Beethoven's nationality. G . . .
8. Composer of the *Royal Fireworks Music*. H . . .
9. Language used for most musical terms. I . . .
10. Holst's 'Bringer of Jollity'. J . . .
11. Composer of *The Sabre Dance*. K . . .
12. Hungarian composer and pianist. L . . .
13. A symphony usually has four of these. M . .
14. Symphony Dvořák wrote in America. N . . .
15. Double-reed instrument. O . . .
16. Italian for 'very softly'. P . . .
17. An English monarch who 'played quite well upon the virginals'. Q . . .
18. Composer of *Bolero*. R . . .
19. Often the third movement of a symphony — Italian for 'a joke'. S . . .
20. Composer of *The Devil's Trill*. T . . .
21. Shostakovich's country. U . . .
22. Elizabethan bowed instrument. V . . .
23. Composer of *Façade*. W . . .

4. Now make up your own alphabet of musical words, giving a clue for each one.

5. Mixed salad

Fill in the dashes to find a mixture of composers, instruments, countries, and titles of pieces of music.

a) H-N-A-Y
b) G-R-A-Y
c) C-RM-N
d) B-RT-K
e) V-OL-N
f) B-S-O-N
g) H-ND-L
h) B-L-R-
i) D-OR-K
j) M-Z--T
k) T-O-B-N-
l) SP--N
M) E-G-A-D
N) C-MB-L
o) T-MP-N-

6. Elimination

When you have arranged the following into matching pairs, *one* word will be left over. Which one is it?

Suite	Gustav	Cor
Symphony	Edward	Horn
Concerto	World	Drum
Spanish	Rimsky	Sabre
French	Capriol	Trill
Anglais	Sleeves	Holst
New	Leningrad	Green
Devil's	Caprice	Elgar
Dance	Snare	Korsakov

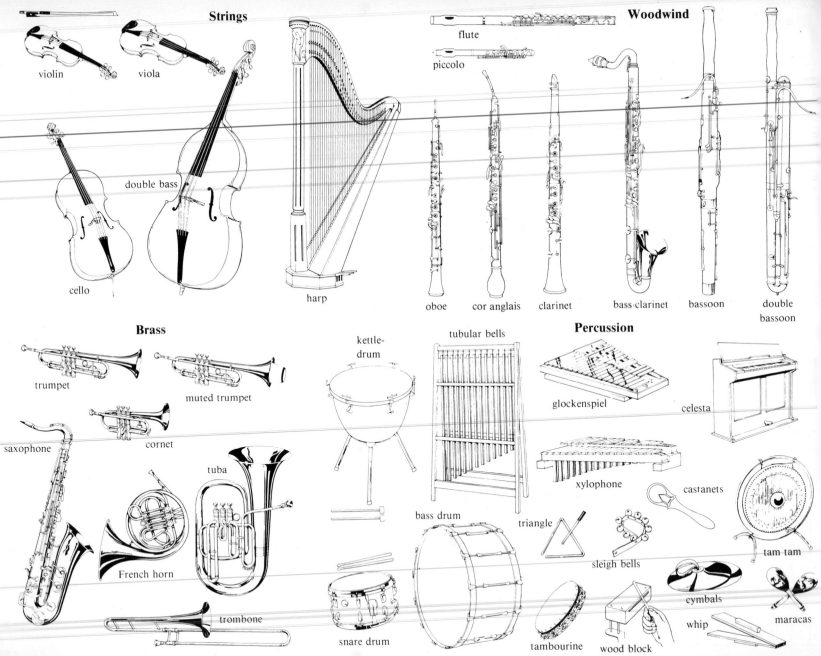

Strings

violin

viola

double bass

cello

harp

Woodwind

flute

piccolo

oboe

cor anglais

clarinet

bass clarinet

bassoon

double bassoon

Brass

trumpet

muted trumpet

saxophone

cornet

tuba

French horn

trombone

kettle-drum

tubular bells

Percussion

glockenspiel

celesta

xylophone

castanets

bass drum

triangle

tam tam

sleigh bells

snare drum

tambourine

wood block

cymbals

whip

maracas